MW00716663

Real Estate Agents, BEWARE!

Real Estate Agents, BEWARE!

Protect Your Deals —
and Increase Your Success —
by Avoiding These Legal Traps

Includes what you need to know about the new Privacy Act

MARK WEISLEDER

ECW Press

Published by ECW PRESS
2120 Queen Street East, Suite 200, Toronto, Ontario, Canada M4E 1E2

NATIONAL LIBRARY OF CANADA CATALOGUING IN PUBLICATION

Weisleder, Mark
Real estate agents, beware! : protect your deals — and increase your success — by
avoiding these legal traps / Mark Weisleder.

ISBN 1-55022-692-4

1. Real estate business — Law and legislation — Canada. 2. Disclosure
of information — Law and legislation — Canada. 3. Real estate agents — Canada.
I. Title.

KE1987.R4W44 2005   346.7104'37   C2004-907044-4
KF2042 R4 W44 2005

Editor: Tracey Millen
Cover and Text Design: Tania Craan
Production and Typesetting: Mary Bowness
Printing: Marc Veilleux Imprimeur

This book is set in Minion.

Passages from the Real Estate Council of Ontario Code of Ethics and the discipline proceedings
related thereto are reprinted with the kind permission of the Real Estate Council of Ontario.

The Ontario Real Estate Association copyrighted forms are used with the kind
permission of the Ontario Real Estate Association.

Although this book discusses legal and ethical situations and principles regarding the
practices of the real estate profession and practitioners, it is not meant to be advice
to the reader about specific legal situations that they may be involved with.
Such readers are urged to consult a lawyer.

The publication of *Real Estate Agents, Beware!* has been generously
supported by the Canada Council, the Ontario Arts Council, the Ontario Media
Development Corporation, and the Government of Canada through the Book
Publishing Industry Development Program. Canadä

DISTRIBUTION
CANADA: Jaguar Book Group, 100 Armstrong Avenue, Georgetown, ON, L7G 5S4

PRINTED AND BOUND IN CANADA

ECW PRESS
ecwpress.com

To Jodi, Hillary, and Jillian,
for always making me appreciate that "these are the days."

To my late parents, Ida and Harry Weisleder,
for their everlasting wisdom.

To Anne, Marsha, and Louis,
for their love and support.

Table of Contents

Acknowledgements

I would like to thank the following people for all their invaluable assistance in helping me complete this book:

Jack and Tracey at ECW Press, for their continuing creative ideas and education;

Don Bastian, for helping me organize my thoughts;

Shaun Belding and Judi Walsh, for their great coaching advice and friendship;

Martin and Ethel Sirotkin, for always being there;

Shelley Koral, Patsy Mackle, and Bob Kinnear at the Ontario Real Estate Association, for their support;

Jeffrey S. Klein, Barrister and Solicitor, for his unique advice on legal claims made against real estate professionals, based on his years of experience as counsel to the insurer for the Ontario Real Estate Association;

Paul Bates, Barrister and Solicitor, for his guidance on what professionals face when confronted with legal proceedings;

All my colleagues at Bell Canada, for their encouragement and for teaching me what a great customer experience is all about.

A Cautionary Tale

There once was a real estate agent who everyone thought was a natural. Let's call him Ted. He was a born people person and always had a smile on his face. He started in the business slowly, acting for buyers while being supervised by experienced representatives in his office. Gradually he began to obtain his own listings and in time proved very successful in closing transactions. As his sales grew, so did his income.

But as he became busier, Ted began to take less care with each of his transactions. He didn't always have the time to complete his paperwork or properly document his clients' instructions. For a while it didn't matter. He was able to use his quick wit and charm to deal with the problems that invariably arose. He was also helped by the fact that he was in an up market and most customers wanted their transactions to be completed, whatever the cost.

Then the market began to turn, and so did the number of listings that Ted had on the go. Unfortunately, he couldn't shake the bad habits he had picked up in the good times: not documenting instructions; not explaining his role to his clients; not following up on items of importance to his client; not being careful in drafting offers; looking the other way when he suspected that his listing clients were not disclosing everything material.

One day Ted signed up a listing with a seller who was noticeably uncomfortable when completing the Seller Property Information Statement. Ted was suspicious that the seller was concealing information, but true to form he did not press him about it. Ted then found a potential buyer for the property. He now had an opportunity to "double end" the entire commission. While the seller was considering the offer, another agent contacted Ted about a different offer for the same property that was $1,000 lower than the offer the seller was considering.

Ted felt that a second offer would only confuse his client this late in the process, and he didn't want to lose the deal he was so close to signing. Besides, the second offer was for less money. He told the second agent that the first deal was already signed by the seller and he could do nothing until the buyers made a final decision. He never told the seller about this offer.

Ted then pressed his buyer clients to make the decision quickly, saying that there might be other offers out there. But the buyers expressed concerns that they might not get approved for mortgage financing because one of them had recently lost a job. Ted said not to worry, and advised them that they could put in a financing condition to protect their interests. So, the buyers signed the agreement.

You can probably see it coming: The bank did not approve them for financing. The buyers wanted to back out of the deal. Ted, however, felt he was in way too far on this one. He stated that he could help them obtain a higher percentage of financing, 90%, by providing an appropriate reference letter to another bank. The letter, written by Ted and not shown to the seller, was a false "gift letter" indicating that the buyers would be obtaining assistance from a relative to help raise the funds necessary to complete the transaction.

The buyers inquired about whether to do an inspection of the property. Ted told them they could rely on the Seller

Property Information Statement, which disclosed no defects. Armed with this information, the buyers closed the transaction. Ted received approximately $18,000 in commissions. However, after the buyers moved in, they noticed many defects in the actual property, all of which would have been uncovered in a normal home inspection. Then they defaulted on their mortgage because they did not have the financial means to carry the property.

The seller, at a party, learned for the first time about the second offer he had never received. He was told that this was just an opening offer and that these buyers would have easily paid another $25,000 for the property.

After the complaints were filed and the legal and discipline proceedings against him were underway, Ted's career came to a crashing halt. No one in his office would speak to him, and his broker was upset that he had to deal with this situation. The ongoing stress caused Ted to lose his health and, ultimately, his ability to earn a living in real estate.

This agent's own actions got him in trouble with what I will refer to in this book as the Real Estate Wheel of Misfortune. But things never have to turn out this way for you. You can be smart, successful . . . and wise. You can avoid some common mistakes or pitfalls, thereby securing your deals. You want to do three things: protect your deals, protect your reputation, and protect your customers. The end result will be a positive, long-term customer base.

IT'S ALL ABOUT LOYALTY

The goal in any business is to obtain and maintain loyal customer relationships. I have often read that the two simple rules of a successful business are:

#1 Keep your existing customers satisfied; and

#2 Get new customers.

As I will demonstrate in this book, these rules are in fact related. If you are successful in keeping your customers satisfied, this will lead them to return to you for repeat business as well as provide testimonials and referrals for potential new customers.

To keep your customers satisfied, you must give them a superior customer experience from the moment you meet with them until the conclusion of the transaction. This means being loyal to your own customers in the manner in which you provide all of your services.

The main goal of this book is to give you the tools to avoid unwanted legal or disciplinary proceedings, which arise when the customer experience that is provided is far from satisfactory. Not only are these unsatisfied customers not going to return to you in the future, but the negative remarks they can make to their circle of friends may have the effect of reducing future business for you in your community.

By following the principles in this book, not only will you avoid these unwanted, time-consuming, non-productive legal or disciplinary proceedings, you will also have the proper foundation and tools to create long-term, satisfied, loyal relationships with your customers that will ensure your continued success.

PROTECT YOUR DEALS

The chief goal of many agents, unfortunately, is to obtain listings. Agents face this pressure every day from their brokers as well as from their own desire to produce income. What they fail to realize, however, is that once you are fortunate enough to obtain a listing, that is when the work really begins. It does not get any easier the more successful you become. Actually, it becomes more difficult, as each client will expect and demand your personal attention.

The best way to protect your deals is to be very organized and meticulous in everything you do on behalf of your client. Be prepared and follow through on every commitment you make. Listen to your customers' needs and take action when required. Keep your customers fully informed at all times about the steps you are taking on their behalf. Do not assume anything.

PROTECT YOUR REPUTATION

The real estate business is largely a word-of-mouth referral process. The successful agent is referred by his clients to other clients on a consistent, ongoing basis. Protecting your own reputation should thus be one of your primary goals in all dealings with your customers. This becomes your personal "brand" or work ethic that you live by every day. This is how you will become known to both your existing customers and potential new ones.

As I emphasize throughout this book, when you are considering following any advice of your client that you do not agree with, or doing anything that you sense is not appropriate, think long and hard about the effect this could have on your reputation if things do not turn out well. All it takes is one problem transaction, complaint, or lawsuit to hurt your reputation, besides causing you great financial and personal stress as you attempt to defend your position.

PROTECT YOUR CUSTOMERS

In every action you take, you should also be focused on properly protecting your customers. This involves everything you do on their behalf, from gathering all the pertinent facts about a property, to completing the agreement of purchase and sale with great care, to following through on the satisfaction of any conditions and any other matters required for closing.

The goal of protecting your customers becomes an important reason for you to take continuing education courses; not only because you will obtain more knowledge, but also because you will be conscious of current issues that may affect your clients, whether positive or negative, and you will have additional tools to protect them. (Keep in mind, you must always draw a very hard line whenever a client asks you to do anything that may be in violation of your applicable Code of Ethics or the law in order to "protect them.")

ABOUT THIS BOOK

This book warns you against approaches and practices that will hurt you as a real estate professional — even to the extent of getting you hauled before your provincial real estate association's disciplinary commission or before the courts. It also gives you advice that will help you become respected, trusted, prosperous, and safe. Aren't these the words you'd like people to use when they talk about you?

Here's how the book lays these topics out:

• Chapter 1 looks at the overarching principle of staying out of trouble through conscientious disclosure practices. Real estate may be all about location, location, location, but for you, personally and professionally, it's all about disclosure, disclosure,

disclosure. This also includes listening to your customers, to
ensure that you have no problems getting paid later.
• Chapter 2 introduces you to the Wheels of Misfortune: the Real
Estate Wheel and the Insurance Wheel.
• In Chapter 3 I help you avoid the "spokes" of the Real Estate
Wheel: the types of activities that can get you into trouble with
your real estate association and with legal proceedings.
• Chapter 4 discusses the new federal privacy act and shows you
how it can become an opportunity for you to market your services
more effectively.
• Chapter 5 closes with tips on risk management – both for keeping out of trouble and for knowing how to act and what to do if
you do get into trouble. I take you through three types of proceedings: legal, real estate association discipline, and privacy.

When explaining real estate discipline proceedings, I use as
a frame of reference the discipline processes and the Code of
Ethics of the Real Estate Council of Ontario (RECO), but every
province in Canada has a similar code and process. In addition, I refer to actual disciplinary proceedings against agents
in Ontario — which, again, are similar to proceedings in the
other provinces.

When the term "agent" or "real estate agent" is used in this
book, I am referring to real estate salespersons who are considered professionals in their field.

Whatever province you practise in, the great thing is that if
you follow the guidelines explored in *Real Estate Agents,
Beware!*, you will protect your deals and ensure your success in
this wonderful profession you have chosen!

CHAPTER 1

It's All about Disclosure, Disclosure, Disclosure

Whenever somebody in one of my real estate seminars asks me an opinion on whether something should or should not be disclosed in a transaction, I usually say: "If you do disclose this, the chances of your being sued will be zero. If you do not disclose this, you may very well not be sued, but there is always the chance. The question that each of you here must ponder is, 'Do I really want to risk a lawsuit?'"

Trouble may come at you from lawsuits brought against you by a seller or a buyer or another agent. But it can also come at you from your provincial real estate association, either through one of their routine checks or because of a complaint filed against you with the association by one of the aforementioned parties.

Obviously, you should try to avoid lawsuits and professional discipline proceedings at any cost. In some cases, as we will see, this may mean saying goodbye to your potential seller or buyer at the beginning of the relationship or partway through the process. Doing so may cost you a commission in the short term, but the peace of mind that you will gain by not having to go through a legal or provincial discipline proceeding will be well worth it.

To put a twist on an existing expression, we should treat our clients, especially in a real estate transaction, as though they were our closest and dearest friends. Putting it another way, if you were the one buying or selling this property for yourself, what would you want to be disclosed to you? Invariably, when I ask agents attending my seminars whether they would want to know the information themselves, almost all of them raise their hands.

If the information is something you would want to know if you were buying the property, then that should be the guideline for full disclosure. Do not confuse full disclosure with privacy legislation. In Chapter 4, "Casting Light on the New Privacy Act," I discuss how full disclosure may or may not be impacted as a result of the new privacy legislation in Canada. For the most part, the principle remains unchanged: Tell your clients everything that you would like to know if you were buying or selling the property yourself.

In some cases, you cannot disclose important material facts. For example, when you are acting in a dual agency situation, you must make it clear at the outset to both parties that you cannot tell the seller how high a buyer may go or the motivation of any buyer in entering into the transaction. However, you are still complying with the concept of full disclosure. You are disclosing fully in advance to your customer what you will not be disclosing, which should protect you from any potential lawsuit or discipline proceeding.

Full disclosure means revealing to your customers the services you will provide and any information about the transaction that affects them. What you will say to third party agents or customers who are on the other side of a given transaction is also encompassed under full disclosure principles.

Real estate professionals are subject to statutory regulation (for example, by the Real Estate and Business Brokers Act in Ontario), as well as by codes of ethics that are adopted by their local Real Estate Association or Council. There are also duties owed to seller and buyer clients that have been established through case law precedents over the years. By following the principles of full disclosure set out in this book, agents are able to satisfy virtually all requirements of any statute, code of ethics, and case law decisions.

GATHERING INFORMATION

In order to make full disclosure in a given transaction, you have to make sure you are gathering all the relevant information as soon as possible in that transaction. Get into the habit of gathering this information the same way every time. It's not easy to document everything you do, but as you'll see later in Chapter 5, "Risk Management," you will have a stronger case, in any legal proceeding, if you can show your normal practice of care in these matters by producing two or three prior customers who can verify that you did follow this procedure during your business relationships with them. This will make it more difficult for a current customer to deny that you followed that process with them as well.

In most cases, the first experience you will have with your customer is when you sign up a potential seller to a listing agreement to sell their property. Proper preparation is key. It is crucial to convey right away to your client the impression that you are very organized and detail oriented and are always there to protect their interests. Before this meeting takes place, you should provide a list of all documents for your seller client to have ready so that the listing process can proceed quickly and efficiently.

Your first step is to review the listing agreement with your customer immediately, so that the customer is aware of all the terms and conditions, including any provisions regarding dual agency.

As will be discussed in Chapter 4 on the new Privacy Act,

this is also an excellent opportunity for you to review your company privacy policy with your customer, to ensure that you have permission to market the fact that you have success-fully sold their property once the transaction has been completed. (See Privacy Principle 8 in that chapter.)

Your next step is to ask the seller to produce whatever doc-umentation they may have about the property so that you can complete the listing information form. This documentation includes the deed, survey, mortgage, and/or tax bill associated with the property. If a survey is available, you may want to walk the property with your client to determine whether or not the survey is up to date, so that you will be able to deal with any survey request that may come with a potential offer on the property.

It is also a good idea to look for the lawyer's report that accompanied the purchase of the property. We live in a time where real estate prices have been gradually rising. It is quite possible that at the time the property was purchased, title or other issues affecting the property were brought to the atten-tion of the buyer enabling them to get out of the transaction. The buyer may have waived these rights due to the fact that the property had increased in value. It's likely that the buyer-now-turned-seller has forgotten the details of those problems. It may not be clear whether title insurance will cover these problems today if they are not disclosed. It is thus important for you to obtain the lawyer's report and review it with your client to determine whether there is anything in it that will have to be disclosed to any potential buyer.

At the initial meeting with your client, obtain all contact numbers, including phone, cell phone, fax, and e-mail addresses where you can reach them. It becomes much easier to demonstrate that you have satisfied the disclosure obliga-tions if you can prove that you did in fact relate the information using some form of communication. If you are in possession of a hand-held pocket computer or similar mobile e-mail device, you can enter the information into it right at the meeting. This also gives you the opportunity to demonstrate to your customer your ability to get in touch with them at any time to keep them updated on the status of their listing. In fact, there are now applications available for these wireless devices that permit you to download all MLS listing information directly to the device. If a customer should ask you the details about what a particular listed property is selling for, you can tell them on the spot not only the asking price for the property, but other details such as square footage and lot size, without having to drive back to your office.

Taking the above-mentioned steps, as part of your initial preparation, will instill confidence in your customers that you have all the necessary tools to provide them with a first class customer experience.

The same preparation is needed when you meet with your buyer customers for the first time. You should go through a complete fact-finding exercise to determine the kind of home they can afford, the area they want to live in, or the need for schools in the immediate vicinity, for example. Are they currently renting a property? If so, you will need to advise them as to how much notice will have to be given in order to properly terminate their lease. Asking questions also demonstrates your caring for the customer, that you are trying to find a home that is best suited for their needs. Not only will this assist you in creating long-term loyal customers, but you will also learn to count many of these customers as future close friends.

SELLER PROPERTY INFORMATION STATEMENT

There has been much debate over whether a seller should sign a Seller Property Information Statement (SPIS) (see Appendix

A). This is, in effect, a type of disclosure that a seller makes about their property — whether they are aware of any defects in the structure, roof, or basement in their property. Some real estate boards in Ontario require that an SPIS form be completed by all sellers and delivered to buyers before an offer is presented. Other boards may not require this, but there is a suspicion that if you do not provide the statement, you must have something to hide. The statement itself is not meant to be a warranty, but allows the seller to indicate property defects if they have knowledge of them.

In my view, the SPIS statement should always be completed by the seller, and the sooner the better. A good time to complete this is at the listing process, when you are gathering information about the property. You can tell a lot by a person's body language. As you go through the statement, watch how the seller reacts when you ask if they are aware of any moisture in the basement or any roof leakage. If you sense that the seller might be lying to you, you should ask yourself whether this is the kind of seller you want to work for. After all, getting out now will save you time and money spent on advertising, conducting open houses, and marketing the sale of this particular property.

Usually, this type of seller will ask you to mislead the buyer. If a legal proceeding is brought against the seller, you can be certain you will be added to the claim, because "you must have known that something was wrong and did nothing to prevent it." Even if you are ultimately vindicated, you will still be dragged through the entire legal process, which means discoveries, cross-examinations, documents, a trial . . . and a lot of stress.

Furthermore, real estate professionals are always wary of customers who use their services and then try to go behind their backs to avoid paying commission, perhaps trying to wait until the holdover period expires. If you suspect that your client is likely to try to cheat a potential buyer, you should immediately be concerned whether he will try to do the same thing to you. And if something does go wrong, this seller will be the first one to blame you. He'll say that he did disclose everything to you and it was your advice not to disclose this to the potential buyer.

You should obtain an SPIS statement for your own protection. It is your proof that you asked the seller questions about the property. With it, you can answer any question that is raised by a potential buyer or purchasing agent. The SPIS is also one of the key documents a lawyer may require in order to properly defend you in an action that may not be commenced until months or years after a transaction has concluded.

Should You Give the SPIS Out?

There is much discussion as to whether you should give the seller property information statement to a potential buyer, since there have been some legal decisions that have relied on this statement as evidence against a seller when problems arose after closing that were not disclosed on the statement.

In my view, the courts are not turning this statement into a seller warranty. The language on the form makes it abundantly clear that when a seller signs the statement, it is for information purposes only and cannot be relied on by a buyer as a warranty for any other purpose. Furthermore, if the seller does not know any given answer, there is no obligation to do any further inspection. The seller can just click the box marked "unknown." However, this does not give the seller the right to actively conceal a defect in a property that could not be discovered in a normal home inspection. Sellers do have legal obligations to disclose these kinds of latent defects, especially when they may render a property uninhabitable by a buyer. If no such disclosure is made, the seller will likely be found liable for negligent or fraudulent misrepresentation after closing, whether or not they supplied an SPIS form, which could lead to a legal claim for damages.

For these reasons, I believe that real estate agents should show the spis form to every potential buyer, especially if they are told in advance by the seller that there are defects in the property. All defects should be disclosed in advance. Some defects may be more material than others, but the logic is still the same: You do not want to risk a lawsuit by not disclosing this information. I would also add that if a buyer raises a concern about any potential defect during the negotiations, and if the matter can be answered by the seller, then it should be included in the relevant space on the spis form. There is nothing wrong with adding an explanation or qualification to any item found on the form. In fact, this should be encouraged, because it serves to bring all potential problems to the attention of the buyer before the agreement is signed.

Remember, if you disclose everything, then it is extremely unlikely that you or your seller will be sued by any buyer. If you do not disclose, there is always the possibility that proceedings will be brought against you as well as your seller client.

Physical and Psychological Defects or Stigmas

Is there any difference between disclosing a physical defect in a property, such as moisture leaking into a basement, and disclosing a psychological defect, such as a suicide having been committed at the property? I believe there is no distinction whatsoever. Psychological defects or stigmas are probably matters that you would like to know about if you were buying the property for yourself.

I have seen a clause that some buyer agents use in this regard. It states:

> The Seller warrants, to the best of his knowledge and belief, that the said property does not contain any hidden defects and that there have been no deaths, suicides, illegal activities, or murders on this property at any time, and that there are no neighbourhood

conditions that could affect the Buyer's use, enjoyment, or perceived value of the property.

The clause is difficult because it's very subjective. What does "neighbourhood conditions" mean? Does it include a group home down the street or on the next block, or perhaps subsidized housing? What if there was a suicide on the property, but it happened four years ago and there have been two ownership changes since? I would not advise any seller to sign this kind of clause, but it does illustrate that people are concerned with psychological issues, which, unlike a leaky roof, have no direct physical impact on a property. We can find out how much it costs to fix a leaky roof. It is much more difficult to determine how much, if any, value is lost to a property as a result of a psychological stigma associated with it.

There was a case in British Columbia a few years ago in which a buyer signed, in November, an offer to purchase a beachfront property. The buyers inquired about the park next door and were advised by the seller that it was a "public beach." When they moved into the property the following May, they were shocked to learn that it was in fact a nudist beach. They then sued for damages. (I know what you are thinking: Wouldn't a nudist beach *add* value to the property?)

The result, after three years of proceedings, including an appeal to the British Columbia Court of Appeal, was that the seller was successful. The seller did not have to disclose this information to the buyer.

The real result, however, was that the seller and the buyer both had to deal with the lost time and stress associated with these proceedings for a three-year period, and the only winners were the lawyers, whose fees totalled more than $100,000. I discuss the legal process and the effects of actual legal proceedings in more detail in Chapter 5, "Risk Management," under the heading "Legal Proceedings."

Will this court decision become an ironclad precedent for any future situation involving a stigma defect? I doubt it. More importantly, do you want to worry about this for three to four years of your life? The answer must be no. My advice, therefore, is to disclose everything that you know to be true, including any of the examples listed above, but do not permit the insertion of the clause itself into any agreement of purchase and sale. Basically, I do not like any warranties given by a seller. I prefer that the buyer satisfies himself about the condition of a property by obtaining a home-inspection report.

A home inspection is the most useful way that a buyer can obtain their own full disclosure about a property. When you act for a buyer, you should always recommend that the buyer obtain a home-inspection report, and you should make the transaction conditional on the buyer being satisfied with the contents of the inspection report, in their sole and absolute discretion. (I discuss the actual wording of the condition in greater detail later in this chapter.) However, you must be very careful when you make this recommendation. Here are some issues to consider:

- Since the buyer will be choosing the inspector, find out who is being chosen to conduct the inspection and complete the report. Are they a certified engineer or builder who can provide a useful opinion?
- Is the home inspector or home-inspection company covered by insurance in the event there is an error in the report that costs the buyer money in repairs after closing?
- If the company is covered by an insurance policy, is there any language in the home-inspection contract that limits the liability of the inspector should anything arise?
- As with most recommendations you make to a client, you should be providing at least two or three reputable names for the client to choose from.

There are regions in Ontario where it has been difficult for home inspectors to obtain insurance protection. Many other inspectors have express language in their agreements that any liability will be limited to the amount of money the buyer paid for the inspection report, which is usually around $500. In most cases, this amount will be insufficient to satisfy any repair damages that may ensue as a result of not finding a problem in the inspection that is discovered later, after closing.

There are also concerns whether having a home inspection completed will negate any representations made by the seller in the SPIS form. In my view, this should not be the case. If a property defect is obvious, then buyers will be deemed to have known about it whether or not they conduct an inspection. So always recommend an inspection. On the other hand, if the defect is concealed, then the seller will still be responsible, despite an inspection having been conducted by a buyer.

There is a growing practice in residential and commercial transactions for sellers to obtain a full inspection report in advance of listing their property.

For the residential property, the inspection would be limited to the physical condition of the property as in a usual home inspection report. In a more complicated commercial transaction, there would be a more detailed structural report prepared by an engineering firm, an environmental report prepared by an environmental consultant, and a financial report, which would comment on the lease income for the property as well as due diligence on the seller's financial records.

Obtaining a home inspection in advance permits buyers to make an offer on the property without the need to make the transaction conditional on obtaining the home inspection in a residential transaction or conditional on structure, environment, and financials typical in commercial transactions. This also brings more integrity to the entire process. Many commercial agents have told me that this process has also generated much more interest in the property on the part of potential buyers, especially institutional investors. From a residential standpoint, this provides the added benefit of not requiring multiple purchasers in a bidding situation from having to conduct costly inspections in advance. They can rely for the most part on the inspection report prepared by the seller.

Although there may be legal issues as to whether the seller must pay extra to have the inspection report create a legal relationship between the buyer and the home inspector, the principal remains the same: Making complete disclosure as soon as possible will not only provide reassurance to any proposed buyer, it should also protect the seller from any unwanted legal proceeding after the fact.

There are now some real estate professionals who will offer to pay for this seller home inspection in exchange for the seller agreeing to list the property with them. This is a very smart practice. Not only does it serve to distinguish this listing professional from others in the area, it gives the listing agent the benefit of knowing in advance the potential problems with the property and they can thus provide the necessary advice to the seller client to make full and complete disclosure.

In order to properly prepare a buyer, you must make it a point to explain the home-inspection process to your client and then let them make all decisions relating to the contract with the home-inspection company as well as the contents of the report. If necessary, also recommend that they obtain legal advice.

It is also imperative that you explain to a buyer client the need to obtain title insurance as part of any transaction. The policy is purchased through the client's lawyer. The main purpose of title insurance is to protect a buyer against title defects or related issues that may not be uncovered by a lawyer who is doing searches for the buyer prior to closing. These include problems with the tax bill owing, zoning irregularities, renovations completed without a building permit, and encroachments onto a neighbouring property. In many cases, these issues cannot be uncovered by a lawyer no matter how careful they may be due to the fact that the survey may be out of date or the municipality's records about the property may not be accurate. They may also include matters that the sellers are not even aware of, so they may not have had any duty of disclosure. Title insurance provides an easy no-fault solution to most of these problems and thus provides peace of mind to most buyers.

Furthermore, a title insurance policy will protect a buyer after closing from the current disturbing trend of third parties attempting fraudulently to take over title to a property without actually paying for it and then borrowing money with new mortgages being registered as security on these same properties. It is a variation on the identity theft problem that is becoming so prevalent today, discussed further in Chapter 4 on Privacy. This can unfortunately occur to anyone, even if you have owned a property and lived there for the past 30 years. The way this is accomplished is that a third party attends the local registry office or goes through the electronic registration system, and registers a false forged deed that transfers title from the real registered owners to the fraud artist. They even pay the required land transfer tax owing. They then approach a bank and apply for a loan, using the same property as security. The bank lends the money and registers a mortgage against the property. The fraudster then disappears and two months later the bank comes to the real owners looking for their money, or else they will be commencing power of sale proceedings. You can imagine the emotional turmoil that this can create. Title insurance will protect the innocent homeowner and will pay all legal expenses to correct the matter, which can sometimes be substantial.

Although banks and lawyers are much more vigilant in

their loan application programs as a result of these events, it still makes sense for buyers to obtain title insurance. In Canada, title insurance companies have now opened up this protection to existing homeowners as well. I recommend that every homeowner contact their lawyer with a view to insuring their titles, to prevent being part of this kind of unwanted legal proceeding in the future.

Your obligations for full disclosure do not end once an agreement of purchase and sale is signed. They continue until a transaction is completed. In the case of *Yorkland Real Estate v. Dale*, the agent did not disclose to her seller client, once an offer was signed, that she had been contacted by a different buyer who was willing to pay more for the property. The agent did not bring this information to the seller, and instead acted on the sale of the property from the initial buyer to the new buyer. Not only did this agent forfeit her commission on the first transaction, she also had to pay to the seller the commission that she earned on the resale as well. All of this could have been avoided if the agent had brought this to the attention of the seller in the first place and just obtained permission to act on the resale transaction.

As many agents are aware, it is very important as a marketing tool to keep your customers informed about market developments and trends even after a transaction has been completed. It demonstrates your willingness to share important information in the marketplace that may concern them and will also keep your name "top of mind" the next time they require real estate services or when they are asked for a referral by someone else. Newsletters are a common way to do this. In Chapter 4 on Privacy, I discuss the way that you can obtain your client's consent in order to continue this kind of marketing once the transaction is completed.

Disclosing Your Services

Full disclosure also means telling the seller or buyer all the services that you will be providing to them, whether you are acting as a listing agent or as a buyer agent. In both cases, care must be taken to review the listing and/or buyer agency agreement at the time you start working with the seller and/or buyer.

You should also be very clear as to how you intend to market the property. Will you be advertising the sale in a newspaper? Will you be sending out flyers? How many open houses will you be conducting? All of this is important information to the seller. You do not want them to have false or unrealistic expectations about the services you intend to provide. Making certain that you have a full understanding of the scope of your duties will help you avoid complaints later on if, for example, the property is not selling as quickly as anticipated.

In Chapter 2, I will introduce the Insurance Wheel of Misfortune, which highlights the basis of the claims that agents have been making to their insurers as a result of commencement of legal proceedings against them. Twenty per cent of all claims are a result of some kind of non-disclosure by the agent. Simply put, this large percentage of claims can be avoided if you adhere to the principle of full disclosure in everything that you do.

Weisleder's Wisdom on . . . DISCLOSURE

1. Be prepared and do your homework before you sign your listing agreement.
2. Make sure the seller has all necessary documents ready before you arrive at the listing.
3. Fill out the SPIS form with your seller.
4. Advise your seller to obtain a home inspection report as soon as the property is listed and provide potential buyers with a copy of this report.

5. Disclose any physical and/or psychological defects to all potential buyers.

6. Be wary immediately of any seller who refuses to disclose pertinent information to a potential buyer.

7. Encourage home inspections for any buyer, as well as title insurance.

8. Check out the background of every home inspector and the home-inspection agreement itself.

9. Disclose all the services you will be providing as soon as possible.

10. Remember that your disclosure obligations continue until the final completion of any transaction.

UNDERSTANDING CONDITIONS

Most consumers believe that if they make a real estate transaction conditional on anything, it is the same as an option to get out of the deal if they are not satisfied for any reason. This is a very dangerous assumption. Interpreting conditions and demonstrating good faith in exercising conditions have been and continue to be the subjects of many legal proceedings.

It is imperative, therefore, that agents understand not only how to compose a condition, but also how to explain the effects of conditions to their buyer and seller customers. When agents complete the standard agreement of purchase and sale, the condition clause is usually the only clause they must draft themselves that is not about just filling in factual details, such as property location, price, or closing dates. This is why you must be extra careful in completing any conditions on behalf of your customers, whether you are acting for buyers or sellers.

As I always say when giving seminars on these topics, I am not a fan of litigation. I believe in settling matters and then moving on. The reason I *am* a fan, even an advocate, of conditions is because they give buyers the time (a) to satisfy themselves regarding any concerns that may affect the property, usually having to do with obtaining sufficient financing; and (b) to complete the purchase and/or home-inspection condition to satisfy themselves as to the physical condition of the property itself.

In most cases, these conditions are for a short time frame, anywhere from three to seven days. Having a property "off the market" for this period of time will normally not materially affect the value of the property. Quite the opposite is often true, as we have seen properties escalate in value in the Toronto area on an almost monthly basis.

Under such circumstances, if a buyer is unsatisfied with the condition, the seller should always let the deal terminate and just move on. I know this is not the attitude many sellers or lawyers take. Many sellers are understandably upset when the buyer attempts to cancel the transaction as a result of the failure to satisfy the terms of a condition. Some sellers claim they want to see a copy of the inspection report, while others want to see proof that the buyers acted in good faith. Can't you just feel the protracted legal proceedings forming?

The case of *Marshall* v. *Bernard Place Corporation*, which was confirmed on appeal in Ontario, is an excellent example. It includes a superbly drafted condition, and it illustrates that no legal position is guaranteed and that most cases result in victories mainly for lawyers, not their clients.

This particular case involved the purchase of a renovated midtown home for $1,510,000. The deposit was substantial: $150,000. The agreement of purchase and sale contained the following home-inspection condition:

This Agreement is conditional upon the inspection of the Property by a home inspector of the Buyer's choice and at the Buyer's sole expense, and receipt of a report satisfactory to him, in his sole and absolute discretion. Unless the Buyer/Cooperating Broker gives notice in writing, delivered to the Seller/Listing Broker on or before Wednesday August 19, 1998, that this condition is fulfilled, this Agreement shall be null and void and the deposit shall be returned to the Buyer without interest or deduction. The Seller agrees to cooperate in providing access to the property for the purpose of this inspection at reasonable times upon reasonable notice given by the Buyer. This condition is included for the sole benefit of the Buyer and may be waived at his sole option by notice in writing to the Seller/Listing Broker within the time period stated herein.

The inspection was conducted and the buyers were not satisfied with the report. They advised the seller on August 17, 1998, that they would not remove their condition and asked for the return of their deposit. The property could only have been off the market for about seven days at most while the inspection was being conducted.

The seller took the position that since the report showed only minor deficiencies, the buyer was not acting in good faith in attempting to satisfy the condition and accordingly were in breach of the agreement itself. They refused to return the deposit, and the matter proceeded to litigation.

Many lawyers were very interested in this case. In fact, the amount of money necessary to correct the deficiencies was very low indeed, about $1,000. In virtually any home inspection, the inspector can make recommendations about needed repairs that will cost at least $500–$1,000, even for minor deficiencies. Most lawyers would probably tell you that the seller had a very good legal position. But this is not what the judge determined, and his judgment was confirmed by the Ontario Court of Appeal.

The main rationale on which the court based its decision was the wording of the clause itself. Since the wording gave the buyer the "sole and absolute discretion" to make a decision based on the inspection report, they had the right to come to the conclusion that they had reached. The outcome of the case may have been different if the buyers had not conducted a home inspection at all, but had just stated that they were not satisfied with the condition of the home. In that instance, the court may have deemed this to have been acting in bad faith. Nevertheless, even though the sellers seemed to have an excellent legal position, the result, after four years of legal proceedings (including pleadings, motions, examinations, production of documents, the trial, and the appeal), ended up costing in excess of $100,000 in legal fees and probably stressed out both sides for the entire four-year period. All because the property was "off the market" for a period of seven days. Or was it "the principle of the matter, not the money"?

The situation described above underscores my point that if you are advising a seller under circumstances where the buyer is attempting to cancel a transaction as a result of a condition, tell them the following: "Let it go. We will get another offer with a buyer who is willing to conclude a transaction. Move on." In the same vein, you should not get too fussed up about the wording of the condition. Some sellers try to remove the words "sole discretion" as a result of the above-noted decision. Others demand to receive a copy of the inspection report. In my view, it is not necessary to spend a lot of time on this kind of negotiation. You want to find buyers who want to complete the transaction with sellers. This is what will give the sellers peace of mind from the time they sign the agreement right through to the closing of the transaction. You do not want to be connected to buyers who are just looking for a way out of the deal. If they can't find an excuse in the wording of the condition itself, they will look for any excuse not to complete the transaction, including objections as a result of the searches conducted by their lawyer. That is not the kind of experience sellers need, especially when they may need the funds from this sale to purchase another property.

I understand some sellers will be concerned that if their property is "sold subject to condition" and then it is later discovered that the condition was not waived, it may lead to negative remarks being made by other agents that "there must be something wrong with the property," and this will make it more difficult to subsequently sell the property to another buyer. Nevertheless, it is still easier to overcome this type of concern by potential buyers than it is to deal with the effects of protracted legal proceedings.

However, when you act as a buyer broker, you must be very careful when drafting your conditions. You cannot assume that your sellers will be accommodating. They may decide to refuse to refund the deposit based on your not acting in good faith or perhaps failing to carry out the terms of the condition.

Questioning Conditions

To avoid problems, it is important for you to understand what should be included in a condition. A properly worded condition should always be at the sole discretion of the buyer, with the right to waiver, and be able to answer the questions: Who? What? How? Where? When?

> What is the subject matter of the condition?
> How is the condition to be satisfied?
> Where is the condition taking place?
> When do you have to notify the other side as to whether you have satisfied the condition?
> Who will be giving the notice?
> Can the condition be waived?

In the condition noted above in *Marshall* v. *Bernard Place Corporation*, all these questions have been answered, as follows:

• What is the subject matter of the condition?

This Agreement is conditional upon the inspection of the Property by a home inspector of the Buyer's choice and at the Buyer's sole expense . . .

• How is the condition to be satisfied?

, . . . and receipt of a report satisfactory to him, in his sole and absolute discretion.

• Where is the condition taking place? Can it be waived?

The Seller agrees to cooperate in providing access to the property for the purpose of this inspection at reasonable times upon reasonable notice given by the Buyer. This condition is included for the sole benefit of the Buyer and may be waived at his sole option by notice in writing to the Seller/Listing Broker within the time period stated herein.

As we learned from the Marshall decision, it is extremely important for you to make the condition for the sole and absolute benefit of buyers. Nevertheless, the buyers must be told that in order to avoid any potential problems, they must still try to satisfy the condition, which in the case of a home-inspection subject matter means they should get a home inspection done. If they do complete the inspection, this clause should give them the ability to get out of the transaction without further incident, so long as they are not satisfied with the report itself.

The reason that the waiver language must be inserted at the sole option of the buyer is to prevent a situation where the condition is not satisfied, but the buyer still wants to go ahead with the transaction. If the waiver is not at the sole discretion of the buyer, then the seller may be able to take the position that they do not agree to waive the condition since it was not satisfied. The seller could attempt this if the property had, for example, suddenly gone up in value from the time the original agreement was signed, in order to escape from the transaction and then re-list the property for a higher price. For this reason, it is always necessary to ensure that the waiver is at the sole discretion of the buyer.

The other popular condition that is used in most transactions is the one related to financing. Again there is confusion as to how a buyer is to satisfy this condition. So long as the buyer makes a legitimate attempt to obtain financing (i.e., goes to a bank for approval), then if they are denied financing, they can terminate the agreement. The clause should still contain the words "sole and absolute discretion," as stated above. There is some confusion as to whether a seller can offer to satisfy the condition by taking back a mortgage from the buyer on similar financial terms. The case law is plain that unless this option is clear from the wording of the condition itself, then this option is not open to a seller under these circumstances. If you are acting for a seller in this situation, remember my advice to just "let it go."

> • Who gives the notice? When do you have to notify the other side?
>
> Unless the Buyer/Cooperating Broker gives notice in writing, delivered to the Seller/Listing Broker on or before Wednesday August 19, 1998, that this condition is fulfilled, this Agreement shall be null and void and the deposit shall be returned to the Buyer without interest or deduction.

This clause could be written in different ways. It could indicate that if the condition is not waived by August 19, then the agreement shall be firm and binding on both parties. Either method is satisfactory. Some drafters like to use the phrase "within five business days of acceptance" as the time period to satisfy the condition. I do not like these words, for they invite confusion. It may not be clear when exactly a contract is in fact accepted, due to many sign-backs that can occur. Also ambiguous is what a "business day" means. Does it include Saturday if, for example, your bank happens to be open on Saturdays? When a definite date is chosen, there can be no confusion.

Waiving Conditions

Claims and complaints have been made against real estate agents as a result of improperly waiving a condition on behalf of a client. This situation can have disastrous results for a buyer. For example, if a buyer does not obtain financing and wants to terminate a transaction, but the agent mistakenly waives the condition, then the seller is clearly within their rights to force the buyer to complete the transaction. Failure to complete may result in the buyer forfeiting any deposit and being responsible for any damages that the seller may incur in reselling the property. RECO discipline proceedings may also arise over this same issue.

In the case of *Nykor* v. *Cil*, decided July 5, 2001, in Ontario, the agent was held liable under court proceedings for damages that were caused to his buyer client as a result of waiving a financing condition prematurely. The agent had to indemnify the buyer for all damages that the buyer had to pay to the seller.

A similar RECO case decided that the action by the agent in waiving the condition without consent from the buyer constituted a violation of Rule 46 of the RECO Code of Ethics relating to unprofessional conduct. The administrative penalty levied against the agent in this disciplinary decision, which also involved other code of ethics violations, was $5,000.

However, we should distinguish this situation from one in which a buyer instructs you to waive a condition even though it has not yet been satisfied. An example would be if the buyer was not yet approved for financing, but was confident that they would be approved since they expected assistance to come from another family member.

In another RECO discipline hearing, dated December 7, 2001, the allegation was that the agent had somehow acted unfairly toward the seller by permitting the buyers to waive a condition about financing when the agent knew that the financing had not yet been arranged. Here's an important statement that came from the decision, which found in favour of the agent:

> In the final analysis, a salesperson will not ordinarily be responsible for a client who, on his own initiative and after due consideration of all material facts, makes the decision to waive a condition included in the Agreement of Purchase and Sale for his benefit.

What can you learn from this? When your client is instructing you to waive a condition without its having been satisfied, you must document these instructions, preferably in a written communication to your client, confirming that you have indeed discussed all "material facts" relating to the decision that has been made. Better still, always have the client sign the waiver themself.

In a rising market, many buyers will instruct you to waive the condition about a home inspection in order to provide a clean offer. This usually involves multiple-offer situations. However, there are other ways to protect the buyer, such as arranging for a home inspection before you submit the offer in the first place. Most sellers will be agreeable to this arrangement. If, however, your buyer has not had a home inspection and instructs you not to include one, or to waive one that has either not yet been completed or satisfied (due to problems that have been identified on the report itself), it is imperative that you document all of these instructions right away. This written record will be critical in any subsequent legal or discipline proceeding.

Speaking of documentation, first and foremost, every agent

must maintain a diary of all significant dates relating to a transaction — one of the most important being the date that a condition expires. Since you may be involved with many different real estate transactions at a given time — closing some deals, negotiating others — it is easy to become confused or forget about these important condition expiry dates. This may cause you to rely on a verbal statement prior to waiving a condition on behalf of your client. Given today's access to e-mails, faxes, and electronic calendars, these verbal statements can easily be avoided.

Prior to waiving any condition on behalf of your client, you should be obtaining written confirmation that the condition has in fact been satisfied. Preferably, this communication should come from your client. It can also come from the buyer's bank, if it's regarding a condition related to financing. One way to easily document these instructions is to have your client e-mail you the instructions, or you can send your client a short e-mail confirming the instructions. As discussed under the heading "Gathering Information" in this chapter, if you have the client's contact information, especially in a wireless mobile device, you can very easily document these instructions in writing.

The bottom line is, if you take the initiative to forward the waiver on behalf of your client, you must take extra care to make sure that you have confirmation that the condition is in fact satisfied before you waive the condition itself. The consequences for a mistake will be costly legal proceedings as well as a potential discipline action by your provincial real estate body.

Weisleder's Wisdom on . . . CONDITIONS

1. When drafting a condition, be able to answer the questions: Who? What? How? Where? When?
2. Insert the words "sole discretion" and "waiver," and ensure that both are "for the sole and absolute benefit of the buyer."

3. When acting for a seller, do not get too hung up on a condition; if a buyer wants to cancel for any reason, let it go.

4. Advise buyers that they must always try to satisfy any condition in good faith.

5. Always keep a record of key condition dates.

6. Always have written confirmation from your client before you waive a condition.

GETTING PAID – HOLDOVER CLAUSES

Probably no issue causes agents more anxiety and concern than customers who make use of their services and then look for a way to avoid paying commission. The listing agreement clearly provides that the owner will pay commission for any sale of the property that occurs during the term of the listing. There is also a holdover clause, which typically lasts an additional 60 to 90 days, specifying that if the seller signs an offer with anyone who was introduced to the property during the term of the listing, then commission is also payable, unless the seller has re-listed the property with another agent.

Historically, sellers have tried to prove that if the agent did not find the buyer, then the agent should not be entitled to commission, even if it was during the listing period itself. For the most part, court decisions have favoured agents on this point. Most sellers in the market now understand this issue. However, when a seller waits out the holdover period and then signs with a buyer who was introduced to the property during the listing period, they have often been successful in resisting claims made by the agent.

It is a different matter when you look at a buyer agency. The buyer agency agreement also contains a clause that if a buyer purchases any property during the term of the buyer agency agreement, then the buyer agent gets paid commission, even if they did not introduce the buyer to the actual property. Most members of the public are not as familiar with this provision. For this reason, it is very important to review the buyer agency agreement carefully with the buyer at the time that it is signed, so that there is no confusion or misunderstanding.

In order to properly manage your risk, conduct this explanation the same way every time, with all of your future sellers and buyers. You should also make a simple note confirming the discussion, either on your own checklist of matters to review with your customer, or as a separate note inserted into your diary or daily planner. Both of these methods can later be used to defend any claim by your customer that you did not explain the document to them in the first place.

Recent decisions involving buyer agency agreements have led to satisfactory results for the agent, when the proper documentation was obtained and then found to have been properly explained. What the cases do not mention, however, is the time it takes when you are involved in a legal proceeding. I want you to be aware of what you will be in for if you bring a claim against a client for commission. I understand the indignation you feel, that someone has cheated you out of a commission. It's costing you money. However, once you read and truly understand what you will face in a court proceeding, I think you may want to think it over some more.

Consider the case of *CB Commercial* v. *Swedcan*, in which a commercial realtor was denied commission. The facts of the case were not disputed. The agent had a listing agreement with a holdover clause. The agent brought in an offer with four days left in the listing period. The seller refused the offer, then signed with the same buyer nine days after the listing expired. This was well within the holdover period. However, the listing agreement also contained the following clause:

> The listing agent agrees to provide the seller with notice of all cus-
> tomers that had viewed the property prior to the expiry of the listing
> period.

The listing agent did not provide an actual list to the seller of all customers that had viewed the property, but relied on the fact that the offer itself constituted notice to the seller of the identity of the buyer. After four long years, the matter was decided in favour of the seller and no commission was paid, due to a strict interpretation of what the notice should have actually contained. If you had asked most lawyers who they thought would have won the action, most would have said the agent. Yet that is not how it turned out.

What I consider even more compelling is that the agent involved in the proceedings now says that he doubts he would ever go through the process again, even if he was certain of a victory, primarily because of the stress associated with the process.

As I discuss in Chapter 5, the legal process is all-consuming, in terms of time wasted and health risked. The time you will dedicate to such an action will be time you are not spending making money. This lost opportunity will more than likely outweigh any monies that you may have lost on the original transaction.

It might help you to look at this issue from a slightly different perspective. In my career at Bell, I have learned two rules when it comes to customer service:

> Rule 1: The customer is always right.
> Rule 2: If the customer is wrong, reread rule number 1.

Here are two examples of these rules in action. My wife is in the clothing business. She told me she once shipped a skirt to a customer via Federal Express. The customer's assistant signed for the package, as confirmed by the courier company, yet the customer insisted she never received it. My wife offered to send another skirt and charge the customer half price. The customer agreed and then badmouthed my wife's business to everyone she knew, which cost my wife future business opportunities in that community.

What if my wife had decided never to trust a customer again? Six months later, another customer purchased an outfit, wore it to a party, and then tried to return it, claiming it didn't fit. Without saying a word, my wife refunded the amount in full. This customer has since referred over a dozen new customers to my wife's business.

The same principles are followed at Bell Mobility, a company known worldwide for having one of the lowest percentages of customers who leave their network. This was not achieved by accident but as a result of a company-wide commitment to listen to their customers and then give the customers what they need.

How does this apply to real estate professionals? They are in a difficult position. The public has an unfair impression that agents do not work very hard and can earn very high commissions for just a few days' work. Unfortunately, when something goes wrong in a real estate transaction, this impression makes the agent the easiest person to blame. Therefore, it is sometimes easy for a customer to justify to himself that he should not pay commission to the agent. The more important issue is how the agent should deal with this situation. The key to remember is: Don't rush to sue or threaten to sue your client.

I recall from my days in private practice that I always dreaded receiving a call from a buyer on the day following closing. They never called to thank me for all the work I did on their behalf. It was always about problems with the new house, anything from damages caused during the moving process to the removal of certain fixtures from the property. It was as though they viewed me as a sheriff who somehow had the ability to pick up the phone and solve their problems in an hour.

One customer complained that the mailbox had been removed. I asked him what name was on the mailbox. He told me it was the seller's name. When I asked why he needed a mailbox with the seller's name on it, he replied, "It's the principle." The same principle was used to explain another customer's anger at light-switch plates being removed — plates which cost probably 50 cents at the hardware store.

Once, a fellow lawyer in our office closed a deal for his own house and came into work stating that the seller had removed all light switches from the wall, so that only a few wires stuck out. They had also taken out all the toilets. Apparently the seller had heard that the buyer was going to demolish the house. What the seller did not hear was that the buyer intended to live in the house for a year before demolishing it. After almost falling down laughing, I thanked him. From then on, whenever a buyer called me after closing to complain about missing fixtures, I always answered, "Just be happy you have your toilets."

I give this example to demonstrate how irrational people can be when it comes to buying or selling a home. For many, it is the single most important and expensive contract that they have ever signed or will sign. If problems arise or if they are just unhappy people, they will try to blame someone and perhaps try to justify not paying an agent commission. This may be their justification in waiting out the holdover period to avoid paying you any commission. If this does happen to you, I strongly recommend that before you rush to sue for your money, you take a step back. Go over everything that you have done for this customer. Did the customer make any complaints while you were working for them? Did you follow through with everything that you said you would do? Were you regularly in touch with the customer, updating them as to the progress of their transaction?

In my experience with customer service at Bell Canada, I have witnessed many complaints from customers. It seems that everyone has some issue with the phone company. It is also my experience that in most cases, you are much better off trying to settle the matter amicably with the customer by trying to understand their position. I like to refer to this as the LAST principle. This stands for:

Listen
Acknowledge
Solve
Thank

Ask your customer to explain why they feel you should not get paid any commission. Sometimes this is all that it takes. The key then is to *listen*. If they do have complaints about you or what you may have done, it is important that you let them explain everything. Do not interrupt. Use words such as "really" or "I see" to show them that you are in fact listening to them, or just nod your head to encourage them to continue. The main thing is to always look interested in what they are saying.

To demonstrate that you have listened, *acknowledge* the customer by repeating the complaint to them. In addition, say something like, "I understand why that would make you upset." Do not admit that you did anything wrong. While you are listening, try to think of an appropriate response that will help *solve* their problem. Finally, always *thank* them for bringing these matters to your attention so that you can benefit from them. If you follow these steps, you have a greater chance of solving the matter in an amicable manner without having to resort to a "demand letter" from a lawyer.

When you solve a complaint in a satisfactory manner, the customer ends up being more loyal to your company than a customer who never had a complaint in the first place. I am sure that you can draw on your own personal experience that when a company went out of their way to satisfy a complaint that you had raised, you probably stayed with that company longer. The same is true of your clients. If you listen to their complaints and then do something about them, it is very unlikely that these customers will have any cause to even think about doing anything to deny you your commission. Not only that, if you are successful in satisfying their complaints, there is still a very good chance that these same customers will refer your services to others through positive recommendations. In this manner, you can use a negative experience to also grow your business.

I understand that there are some customers who may be completely dishonest, who never had any intention of paying you. You are correct to feel you want to teach them a lesson so that they don't try to do this to you or anyone else again. But also realize that anyone who is completely dishonest will continue to do everything possible to avoid paying you anything. This could include hiring their own lawyer who will delay the proceedings as much as possible. Undoubtedly, you will become emotionally consumed with the lawsuit. Besides taking away from your ability to earn more commissions, it may also have a negative impact on your reputation, as people will hear that you are in court over non-payment of a commission. People will wonder why someone did not want to pay you, and might start questioning your competence. You do not want customers or potential customers to be thinking this about you or your services.

Even if as a result of your trying to resolve the matter amicably you are not able to do so, it is not a complete loss. You can still learn something from this experience. You will be better able to recognize a similar type of seller in the future, and you will make sure that you are better prepared for every customer interaction. No experience is a failure if you learn something valuable from it.

If you follow the principles in this book, there should be no reason why a customer would ever feel that you do not deserve to be paid. If this does occur, however, remember also to use the experience positively, instead of bristling and heading down the road of uncertain, expensive litigation.

Weisleder's Wisdom on . . . GETTING PAID

1. Review your listing and buyer agency agreements carefully with your clients, especially the holdover clause.
2. Follow through on all your commitments and keep the customer informed.
3. Listen for any concerns or complaints raised by your client and then solve them.
4. Resolve any problems using the LAST principle.
5. Do not rush to sue someone when things go wrong; learn from every bad experience instead.
6. Remember, satisfying complaints can lead to further referrals; turn the negative experience into positive results.

CHAPTER 2

The Wheels
of Misfortune

There are two wheels of misfortune, and you never want to find yourself hurt by either of them, whether out of ignorance, negligence, or attempts to get around your provincial council's code of ethics. They are the Real Estate Wheel of Misfortune and the Insurance Wheel of Misfortune. Following are two pie charts that have been compiled by the underwriter for the errors and omissions policy of the Ontario Real Estate Association (OREA) and by the Real Estate Council of Ontario (RECO), showing, by category, the kinds of RECO discipline committee claims made against real estate agents and the kinds of errors that lead to lawsuits and thus claims against an agent's insurance policies.

In the next chapter I will discuss some of these "spokes" of the Real Estate Wheel of Misfortune, and what you should be aware of when you are doing business as an agent. By following key rules and guidelines, not only will you avoid any unwanted discipline proceedings, but you will also avoid any associated claims against your insurance policy. Note that while OREA and RECO rules are discussed throughout this book, most provincial bodies dealing with real estate follow similar rules and practices so the principles are applicable wherever you may practise.

Real Estate Wheel of Misfortune

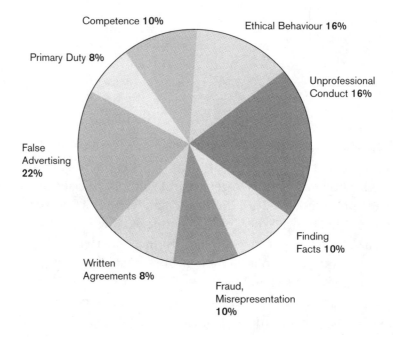

Competence **10%**

Ethical Behaviour **16%**

Primary Duty **8%**

Unprofessional
Conduct **16%**

False
Advertising
22%

Finding
Facts **10%**

Written
Agreements **8%**

Fraud,
Misrepresentation
10%

Your goal is to conduct yourself as an agent, and to do business as an agent, so that you never get into trouble with your provincial association's Wheel of Misfortune, and so that you are never exposed for ignoring, flouting, or not knowing any of these rules.

THE REAL ESTATE WHEEL OF MISFORTUNE

The Real Estate Council of Ontario has established a code of ethics for its members. The purpose is not only to ensure that agents deal with each other in good faith, but also to protect the public. To enforce and ensure compliance with this code of ethics, RECO has established through a by-law a discipline committee whose members are appointed by the RECO board.

The code of ethics is made up of 50 rules, of which 23 have not yet been allocated. That leaves 27 rules, which, if breached, could conceivably make you the subject of a RECO discipline committee hearing. For each rule, there are guiding principles to provide examples and amplification of the code of ethics. In order for RECO to accept jurisdiction and process the complaint, an agent must have violated one of the rules under the RECO code of ethics.

I have included references to the applicable rules of the current Ontario Code of Ethics in Chapter 3 where I discuss the consequences of each rule. Similar codes are found with the other provincial real estate boards. It is expected that these rules will eventually be incorporated into the public statutes that govern real estate agents in general for all provinces. In Ontario, for example, the government has already circulated a proposed draft code of ethics for comments by all interested stakeholders, which would incorporate the main principles of the current code of ethics into the Real Estate and Business Brokers Act statute that would govern all real estate brokers and agents in Ontario. It thus becomes increasingly important for agents to know what is expected of them under these rules.

In all areas where agents are making errors that end up with legal proceedings, they constantly involve a violation of one of the code of ethics rules. This applies in all jurisdictions

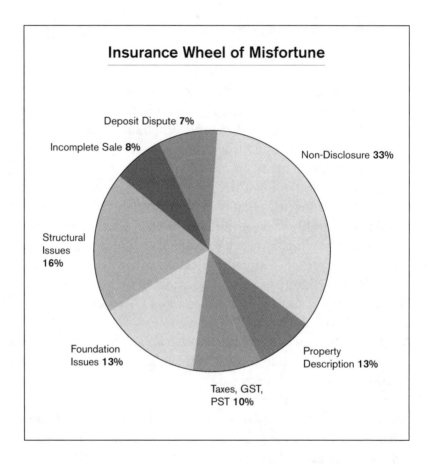

Insurance Wheel of Misfortune

Deposit Dispute **7%**

Incomplete Sale **8%**

Non-Disclosure **33%**

Structural
Issues
16%

Foundation
Issues **13%**

Property
Description **13%**

Taxes, GST,
PST **10%**

in Canada where agents do business. Similar codes of ethics are also found in every state in the United States, illustrating that these principles apply to all real estate professionals who practise anywhere in North America.

THE INSURANCE WHEEL OF MISFORTUNE

On the insurance chart, you can see the types of claims that agents have had to report to their insurers in Ontario as a result of claims made against them. These claims fall under the insurance company's errors and omissions policy. The errors or omissions that are being made are most often a result of not following the principles under the code of ethics. In many instances, it is just about not being careful. Yet this behaviour can quickly lead to claims about negligence. In effect, we can see how both Wheels of Misfortune intersect — if you manage to conduct yourself in a manner that keeps you out of trouble with one of the wheels, you will almost automatically stay out of trouble with the other wheel as well.

AN OVERVIEW OF HOW REAL ESTATE COUNCIL PROCEEDINGS WORK

Once a complaint is made against you in writing to your provincial real estate council, either by a member of the public or another agent, it will be reviewed to determine whether any further action is necessary. In Ontario, if the complaint refers to a violation of the RECO Code of Ethics, then RECO will accept jurisdiction and deal with the matter. If it is beyond their jurisdiction, they will refer the matter to the appropriate body, such as a local real estate board, and RECO will close the file.

Once jurisdiction is established, RECO will notify the agent that it has accepted jurisdiction and the agent then has 15 days to respond to the allegations that have been made. The broker that employs the agent will also be contacted. A researcher may be appointed to investigate the matter on behalf of RECO, and the agent will be asked whether he consents to be interviewed by the researcher.

The role of the researcher is to gather information so that the manager appointed under the process can make a screening decision as to whether to refer the matter to a discipline committee hearing, use an alternative forum for resolving the matter, or simply close the file. The protection of the public interest is the guiding factor in deciding which recommendation to make.

If the matter proceeds to a hearing, three committee members will be appointed to hear the case and make a decision. The agent is given 30 days' notice prior to the hearing itself. The agent will be issued a copy of all written documentation that RECO intends to rely on at the hearing, including a statement as to which rules of the code of ethics have been violated and the factual basis for the claims made. The agent must file any evidence that they wish to produce at the hearing, whether documentary or testimonial, at least 15 days prior to the hearing. In this manner, there is an attempt to have full disclosure of each side's position to the other side prior to the actual hearing.

RECO will present all evidence at the hearing, including the witnesses that it intends to rely on. The agent will have the opportunity to cross-examine any witnesses who attend, as well as to present their own evidence. The decision of the panel is then forwarded to the agent within ten days of the hearing.

If an alternative dispute resolution mechanism is selected, the parties are required to cooperate in trying to reach an agreement on how to resolve the matter. If an agreement is reached, it still must be approved by the manager assigned to the file, for the protection of the public interest.

In order to appeal the decision of the committee, under a RECO hearing, you must file a notice of appeal within 30 days of receiving the decision. To win the case on appeal, the agent must be able to prove that the committee had no jurisdiction to hear the matter or that there was a denial of natural justice, for example if the committee members were biased against the agent.

Failure to comply with the decision of the committee will result in the immediate termination of an agent's membership with RECO and registration as an agent under the Real

Estate and Business Brokers Act. In other words, you are out of business.

In the case of *Luzak* v. *The Real Estate Council of Ontario*, decided October 9, 2003, the agent went through the discipline committee hearing process and was given a penalty of $6,000 and costs of $1,000, which he appealed. The appeal committee that was appointed to hear the matter included a member who also had been on the original panel that heard the complaint. The agent felt that this would bias the appeal committee against him and thus requested that a different panel be appointed. RECO denied his request, so the agent took the commission to court to argue that this constituted a denial of his right to natural justice.

The court found that the agent did not offer any evidence proving that RECO's conduct in not replacing the member denied him the right to natural justice or was unfair to him. He had been duly notified of the complaint made against him and he had received an impartial hearing. The decision was also noteworthy because it provides a judicial stamp of approval to the entire process by which RECO was set up to enable the real estate profession as a whole to be self-governing. This gives RECO the right to pass by-laws to ensure that its members comply with its code of ethics, all for the protection of the public interest.

RECO does not take this obligation lightly, which is why it has strict requirements about the membership qualifications and educational standards for all of its members. This same principle applies to all other provincial real estate association bodies that have been formed to monitor and regulate the real estate profession and professionals in their areas. In the United States, these same obligations and discipline type proceedings are still carried out by the state regulatory bodies, and have not been delegated to the real estate profession. However, the principles applied in the discipline decisions in these states are very similar to the principles found in the codes of ethics and the decisions arising out of the codes of ethics across Canada.

Based on my review of the decisions involving RECO, I can say that it is best for the agent to be very cooperative with the process as soon as he receives the initial notification. If the matter can be resolved through alternative dispute resolution, this is the preferred route to take. This will dispose of the matter much more expeditiously, minus the stress and uncertainty that accompanies the hearing process.

My advice, if you do proceed to a hearing and a decision is reached, is that you do not appeal the matter. Virtually all appeals are unsuccessful, as it is extremely difficult to prove that the committee was biased against you. The committee members are fellow real estate professionals who understand the business and take their responsibility very seriously. They review all facts presented and consider all arguments before rendering any decision.

AN OVERVIEW OF HOW TO WORK WITH YOUR INSURER

Once you receive a letter or legal claim from anyone that could result in damages claimed, you must immediately inform your insurer. It is best to let them determine the course of action that they wish to take.

If you make any admission of liability before contacting the insurer, there may be grounds for the insurer to deny coverage. Although you may be tempted to try to settle the matter yourself, to make it go away, do not consider this option for the same reason: that the insurer may be able to use this as a reason to deny coverage.

Let your broker know immediately about the complaint or letter that you have received. You may also want to get legal advice before acting. The key thing to remember is not to act quickly in this situation. When someone makes an allegation that you are not competent in your chosen career, it can cause severe personal and professional stress. You are in no position to decide how to proceed. That is why you should contact the insurer first. As long as they are making the initial decisions as to how to proceed, there is virtually no way that they can deny coverage later, unless the complaint is part of the exclusions under their policy.

Once the insurer gets involved, a claims manager or adjuster will take charge of the file and determine how to proceed. This could involve recommending a quick settlement with the person making the claim, if the situation warrants. A decision could also be made that the matter needs to be defended, and the claims manager will then appoint a lawyer to act on the insurer and the agent's behalf.

An ounce of prevention being worth a pound of cure, it is best to find out how to avoid any kind of hearing at all. To do this, you must understand the rules of the code of ethics, which are explained in the next chapter.

Beware the Spokes of the Real Estate Wheel of Misfortune

This chapter focuses on the key code of ethics rules that serve as a guide to appropriate professional conduct in the course of carrying out business. When an agent violates one of these rules, it results in unfavourable consequences for the agent or a member of the public. If you follow the "Weisleder's Wisdom" principles at the end of my discussion of each rule, you will avoid being hurt by one of these spokes.

In my experience, almost every legal claim made against an agent is caused by crossing the line on one or more of these code of ethics rules. By avoiding getting hurt by the spokes of the Real Estate Wheel of Misfortune, not only will you be conducting your profession in a safe and respectable manner, you will also be avoiding the disciplinary or legal claims that could destroy your reputation as well as your ability to earn a living. At the same time, you will be practising in a manner that instills trust and confidence in your customers, which will lead to long-term loyal relationships and referrals.

Please note that I do not discuss every rule in the Ontario code, nor do I discuss them in the order in which they appear in the code. I have tried to get at the most important points, in an order that fits the concerns of real estate professionals wherever they may practise.

The cases referred to in the following pages are based on

discipline committee proceedings commenced in the province of Ontario, yet the principles to be learned apply equally to all jurisdictions across Canada. All cases can be viewed in their entirety online at the RECO Web site, www.reco.on.ca, under the subheading "Discipline Proceedings." (This is another reason not to get into trouble with your local real estate association. Your name and thus your reputation will become exposed to everyone who has access to the Internet, to observe the details of your particular decision.)

Ethical Behaviour (Rule 1)
A Member shall:
1. endeavor to protect and promote the best interests of the Member's Client,
2. endeavor to protect the public from fraud, misrepresentation, or unethical practice in connection with real estate Transactions,
3. maintain and enhance the Member's degree of skill and competence,
4. render services, including giving advice and opinions, based on the Member's training, qualifications, and expertise,
5. deal fairly, honestly, and with integrity with the public, other Members, and third parties,
6. cooperate with the Council in fulfilling its duty to serve and protect the public interest,
7. comply with the Real Estate and Business Brokers Act and the regulations under it and by the laws of the Council

Guiding Principles
1.1 Ethical behaviour is based upon the Golden Rule: "Do unto others as you would have them do unto you."
1.2 The opening words to this rule are taken from the requirements imposed on all Members by subsection 6(1) of the Real Estate and Business Brokers Act. The Code of Ethics is a description and amplification by the Council of this obligation.

1.3 Members are expected to keep abreast of the current profes-
sional standards.
1.4 The Code of Ethics set the minimum requirements that
Members are expected to meet.
1.5 This Code of Ethics shall apply to all Members despite any
agreement to the contrary.

The concept of the Golden Rule is found in almost all codes of ethics that I have reviewed, including the code of ethics of the U.S. National Association of Realtors. It is a simple yet power-ful lesson.

In virtually every discipline decision that has been success-fully brought against an agent anywhere, one of these subsections of Rule 1 has been violated. In every decision that you will make, whether it is related to advertising, duties to your clients, disclosure to your clients, or discovery of facts, you will always be faced with the ethical dilemmas as to what should guide your actions. This rule becomes even more important in the real estate profession, where an agent's name in the community is one of the primary marketing tools that he or she uses to earn a living.

Major corporations spend a lot of money on their brand image — what sets them apart from the competition. Many corporations have learned the hard way that their business suffers whenever they sacrifice that brand image in order to make a fast profit at the expense of their customers. They may make their financial statements look a little better in the short term, but they lose a lot more — customers, repeat business, referrals, goodwill — over the long term.

Rogers Cable, the leading cable provider in Ontario, once attempted to introduce a service through negative option billing, whereby they provided their customers with five or six new channels for a three-month period in order to try them out. What they did not tell their customers was that they would automatically be charged an extra monthly fee in the fourth month if they did not call in to cancel the service. This was clearly an attempt to raise short-term revenues, banking on the probability that many customers would not think to call and cancel the new service. However, this led to a public outcry so severe that Rogers immediately changed their policy.

The damage caused to the Rogers brand was significant. Over five years after the incident, I noticed the following headline in a newspaper article in Toronto: "Negative Option Billing Rises to New Heights in Toronto." When I saw the headline, I thought that Rogers had made the same mistake involving negative option billing. I was surprised to learn that this article was actually about Rogers' decision to relocate to a new office tower in downtown Toronto. The negative term used to describe this innocent business move demonstrates how a company error can do long-term damage to that same company's reputation and brand image.

The same principle can be applied directly to the real estate business. Do not be tempted to cross the line, in order to make a deal happen, just because the commission can be very lucrative. Look at the long-term cost. When I was in private practice as a lawyer, clients would sometimes ask me to cross the line on a transaction. My response usually went like this: "I am sorry that you think that my licence to practise law is only worth $500, which is the fee that I will earn on this transaction." (Now, had the fee been $5 million . . . you can see the temptation.) That is what you will be risking when you cross the ethical line. As for agents who have ever been caught in a disciplinary or legal proceeding as a result, their answers are always the same: It wasn't worth it.

Another brand lesson to be learned is that it is not advisable to attack your competitor's brand. Instead, just show why you are different. Show the benefits your organization brings. Pepsi took on the world's most popular brand, Coke, in the

famous "taste test" advertising campaign. For a while they succeeded, so much so that Coke changed their formula. (I am
told that this came about after the Coke board of directors
took the Pepsi taste test and voted for Pepsi.) Reaction to the
new Coke was a disaster. They got the message and reintro-
duced the original formula, as Coke Classic, and have never
looked back.

Toys "Я" Us is one of the strongest children's toy brands in
the world. A new company, called SmarterKids.com, entered
the market and tried to do things a little differently. They
developed a gift centre online so that relatives could avoid
giving the same present as other relatives. They permitted a
child's profile to be entered so that gifts could be recommended to suit the particular child. This company was
successful not because it claimed to be better than Toys "Я" Us,
but because it demonstrated how it was different.

It is tempting in the real estate business to bad-mouth
another agent since many agents usually compete for the same
listings. This is clearly a dangerous practice and a violation of
the ethical behaviour rule. Consider the discipline case of
Holliday, decided August 14, 2002. The complaint was made
that this agent attacked the reputation of another agent. The
attacks included the claims:

> • that although this other agent had a lot of listings, he did not
> sell many properties because he offered selling agents commis-
> sions that were too low;
> • that the high number of listings carried by the agent meant he
> was too busy to provide proper service to his customers;
> • that their actual sales in the area were much lower than other
> agents; and
> • that this broker would be out of business within six months.

All of these claims were deemed false and misleading. Not only were they deemed to be a violation of Rule 10 (Misrepresentation), they were judged a violation of this rule, specifically Rule 1.5, in that the actions were not considered fair dealing with other members of the profession and the public.

The power of e-mails and the Internet makes it more important than ever to satisfy your customers' complaints. Consider the following example from outside the real estate business.

Two consultants tried to check into the Doubletree Hotel in Houston after midnight. They were told that they had lost their room, even though the room had been guaranteed in advance by credit card payment. So, the consultants decided to strike back. They prepared a short PowerPoint presentation indicating their displeasure and sent copies of it via e-mail to a few of their friends. The presentation contained charts and graphs, which consultants love to use, showing, for example, how much business the hotel would lose based on the negative word of mouth that would result from the consultants' negative experience.

Suffice it to say that within a few weeks, this e-mail had been forwarded throughout the hospitality industry. It has even become part of a course at a major U.S. university as an illustration of how you should not treat a customer. This incident caused Doubletree International to issue a formal statement explaining what had occurred.

The moral of the story? You should always take customer complaints very seriously. If you are not listening to your customers and satisfying their needs, complaints will result. Perhaps the complaint may not go as far as a discipline hearing or a lawsuit. But it will definitely be made to other members of the community — and that will tarnish your own personal brand.

So many times we are tempted for the sake of expedience to cross the line. In the discipline case of Ip, decided March 14,

2002, the agent signed the names of his clients on documents instead of taking the time to get the clients to do so themselves. The complaint was raised by the broker, who formerly employed this agent, due to irregularities in the transaction. The agent stated that he was "verbally instructed to do so." He was trying to keep his clients happy, as this is what he "knew they wanted." The sellers even sent letters stating that they were happy with the results obtained. It was nevertheless held to be a violation of Rule 1, Ethical Behaviour. The fine levied was $2,500 and costs came to $2,100.

Do not be tempted to initial the customer signatures during signbacks as offers go back and forth. You may think you are doing your client a favour by initialling documents on their behalf, based on a verbal instruction, but you are not. Without written authorization, you are headed for a problem. What if your client changes their mind after the signing takes place? They will quickly point to the final initial and state that this was not their signature, that they had not authorized the change.

I recall a similar situation when I was starting out in private practice. A client needed a document notarized. It is required that the client sign a document in the lawyer's presence before the notary stamp can be affixed. The client, however, did not want to travel downtown just to sign the document. They asked if they could just tell me they signed it and courier it downtown, where I could then affix my notary stamp and send it back to them. What I did was I called the client and told them that I had to be in their neighbourhood anyways and I would come and see them to sign the document. It was easier to explain the legal requirements about signing the documents when I was at their office. This also gave me the opportunity to meet them at their place of business, and they subsequently gave me a tour. I learned a lot more about my client's business, which led to a greater amount of work from them in the following years.

The above-noted example took a potential negative situation, which was going to inconvenience the client, and turned it into a positive experience for everyone, while at the same time educated the client about the reasons for the ethical and legal requirements. This client not only became a valuable client, but I remain close friends with them today.

Part of being properly prepared when presenting an offer is knowing at all times how to reach your client. Educate them in advance that offers may be signed back and forth during the day or night and they must be available so that any changes can be properly reviewed. If this is properly explained ahead of time, the client will not be upset about meeting you to do any final initials; rather, they will appreciate and respect your professionalism. This confidence in your abilities is what leads to more referrals later. The customer who *is* impressed with cutting corners is the kind of customer that you should not be acting for in the first place. You do not need those kinds of referrals either, as they will ruin your reputation in the long run.

In a world where we can communicate almost instantaneously with our customers, there is no reason why we cannot obtain appropriate written instructions and authorizations when needed. Always use your contact information to keep the customer informed, especially by e-mail, as virtually all customers now have an e-mail address.

I am not a big fan of customers who expect an agent to cut commissions in order to get the deal done. Some people feel that agents are overpaid and do hardly any work and thus should not be upset if they are asked to cut their commissions. But this request should not arise if you have done an appropriate job of demonstrating your professionalism at the time you obtain the listing or the buyer agency agreement, and if throughout the process you listen to your customers and satisfy their needs.

You need to develop a policy of what you will do if this request does arise, and that policy should be to just say no. Cut your commission once and the word will get around, and you will always be asked to cut your commission. It may be better to let one deal go by refusing to comply with such a request than to create this kind of reputation.

However, if you do agree to rebate the commission, for any reason, then you must follow through on your commitment. In the discipline case of Szewczyk, decided October 3, 2003, the agent offered to rebate 1% commission to the buyer in order to make the deal happen. But he did not follow through on his promise, trying to explain himself to the customer by saying he was having financial difficulties brought on him due to the actions of third parties. The penalty in this case was severe, $12,000, with costs in the amount of $1,750. The agent did not pay the penalty and subsequently lost his licence and registration.

The discipline proceeding of Sheppard, dated April 10, 2002, is instructive. This agent tried to seal a deal by making personal guarantees to the seller that if the buyer defaulted on the deal, he would back it up. In this way he convinced the seller to give the buyer additional extensions to complete the transaction. The facts of this case were complicated, but it became clear that as neither the buyer nor the agent was able to satisfy the purchase commitment, it led to one misleading event after another, until the lawyers came running.

The agent was deemed to have violated Rule 1 above all, by giving a guarantee without the financial ability to satisfy it. This resulted in a penalty of $12,000 and costs of $1,800 against the agent.

In another discipline case, one involving Ebrahim, dated January 9, 2002, the agent tried to put her own money into the deal to help secure extensions. She hoped these extensions would permit the buyer to come up with the money to complete the transaction, or enable her to find another buyer to complete the transaction. Although the agent meant well, she would have better served her seller customer right from the start by letting them know the buyer was having difficulties and then letting the seller make the decision as to what to do. The result not only cost the agent the money she had put into the transaction, which was forfeited, but also a penalty of $2,000 and costs of $1,100.

If you are acting as a listing agent, be sure to ask a buyer if they are already being represented by someone else. Buyers will be very tempted to say no if they think this will result in a lower price to be paid for a property that they may find on their own.

The discipline case of Middleton, decided January 25, 2002, illustrates this concept. The agent was deemed to have violated Rule 1 by not informing the buyer agent what was going on when the buyers tried to complete the transaction directly with the listing agent without informing the buyer agent. The listing agent took the position that the buyers were not happy with the buyer broker service and he was only trying to satisfy the customers' wishes.

The committee ruled, however, that once the agent knew that a buyer broker was involved, he had to satisfy himself that the buyer broker was made aware of the situation so that the matter could be resolved with all appropriate parties involved. The penalties were $3,000 each against both the listing agent and the listing broker, with costs of $1,950 against each party as well.

In the same vein, a listing agent must be careful to tell a client and potential buyers about every potential offer, and not to try showing only offers where the agent is receiving commissions from both the seller and the buyer. In the discipline case of Stephenson, dated October 12, 2001, the listing agent did not disclose to the buyers that there was another offer involved where the listing agent was also acting for the buyer. This would have considerably affected the price that the second buyer might have contemplated. Failure to disclose this information was held to be a violation of Rule 1, as the agent stood to profit from this non-disclosure and it could also have compromised the ability of his own seller client to obtain the highest price for the property. The fine was $5,000 and costs were $1,000.

In the discipline case of Lee, dated August 3, 2001, it was alleged that the agent, who left one broker for another, had attempted to have her former listing sellers cancel their listings with her former employer so that she could sign them up with her new employer. Not only was it found that she had interfered with her former broker's contractual relationships with these sellers, she had also put these same sellers at risk by having them sign new agreements with her current employer before they had been properly released from their earlier agreements. The fine in this case was $5,000 plus costs of $1,300. In deciding the penalty, the panel took into account the fact that the agent admitted that what she did was wrong and felt regret for her actions.

Claiming that you made a mistake, especially if it was a careless one, is not an answer to an allegation that you have violated this rule on ethical behaviour. The rule makes clear that you must be always up to date on current standards. In the discipline case of Ferri, decided March 19, 2002, the agent was careless in not checking the status of a basement apartment prior to renting it out for an owner. Had it been checked, the agent would have learned that the apartment was not permitted under the city by-laws. It was not a defence by the agent that "most agents did not know about this by-law." Although there was no intent to deceive anyone, this careless act of the agent resulted in a violation not only of the rules regarding advertising, but also of this rule on ethical behaviour. The penalty imposed was $500, with costs of $1,650.

Part of ethical behaviour includes not taking shortcuts. An example would be where you decide to reduce a sale price on a listing without obtaining confirmation in writing from your seller. Many agents just do this based on verbal instructions. In the case of Thomson, decided March 1, 2001, the agent changed the listing price without written confirmation because it was "inconvenient to do so." As you can imagine, the seller later complained that they did not remember having authorized this change and there were confusions as to the prices that should have been listed. The penalty imposed was $1,000. All of the confusion as well as the subsequent proceeding could have been avoided if a little more time was taken to obtain the change in writing directly from the client.

Another example is following through on what you say you will do. In a case dated November 21, 2002, the agent represented to the seller that they would take out advertising in a particular publication called the *Real Estate News and Buyers Guide*. Advertising was done in another medium instead. The agent argued that he did provide the seller with equivalent advertising. Although the parties verbally discussed potential alternatives, nothing was reduced to writing. It was found that the agent was in breach of Rule 1 in not following an express term of the listing agreement. If there was to be an alteration, it had to be done in writing. The penalty in this case was $1,000 and $900 in costs.

In attempting to sum up the ethical behaviour obligation, the proposed new Code of Ethics for the Province of Ontario suggests that every agent shall treat every person in the course of a trade in real estate "fairly, honestly, and with integrity." I could not have summarized this duty any better. This is also the cornerstone of providing loyalty to your own customers. If you want your customers to be loyal to you, you must also demonstrate this kind of loyalty to them. Follow this advice and you will avoid violating virtually all of the rules in any code of ethics.

Weisleder's Wisdom on . . . ETHICAL BEHAVIOUR

1. Your reputation or brand image is a valuable asset; protect it at all costs, even if it means losing a commission.
2. Do not disparage the name of another agent; instead, show how you are different.
3. Never try to save a transaction by providing a guarantee or contributing any financing.
4. Do not take any shortcuts, whether in taking instructions or preparing documents. Confirm all instructions in writing.
5. Always follow through on all of your written commitments, especially what you have agreed to on your listing agreement.
6. Demonstrate and explain your professionalism at all times.
7. Always ask yourself, "Is this worth losing my licence, or being involved in a discipline or legal proceeding?"
8. Do not attempt to take a customer away from an existing relationship with another agent. If people know you are good, they will find you the next time.
9. Be loyal to your customers in everything that you do, and they will be loyal to you in the long term.

Unprofessional Conduct (Rule 46)
A Member shall not engage in an act or omission relevant to the practice of the profession that having regard to all of the circumstances, would reasonably be regarded by Members or the public as disgraceful, dishonourable, or unprofessional.

Guiding Principles
46.1 A Member should only act on the authority of the Member's Client. Authority should be written, verbal, or implied. A Member should obtain written authority whenever practical.

46.2 A Member should not practise when impaired, by alcohol, drugs, or any other substance.

46.3 A Member's conduct should be professional with other Members or outside professional advisers.

46.4 A Member should not directly or indirectly benefit from the practice of the profession while the Member's registration is suspended, unless the Member first adequately discloses the nature of the benefit to the Council and obtains the prior written consent of the Council or a Committee of the Council.

46.5 A Member should not permit or assist a Member whose registration has been suspended or revoked or whose registration the Registrar has refused to renew from directly or indirectly benefiting from the practice of the profession.

Unprofessional conduct is another rule that is so foundational it invariably is violated together with many of the other rules. Although most principles of this rule are straightforward and sound like common sense, it's amazing how quickly they can be ignored in the pursuit of the next commission.

Situations arise in which, as a result of your participation in a transaction, you may be paid commissions or incentives from various parties, or you may decide to invest in part of the transaction yourself. There is nothing inherently wrong with making this profit, as long as there is complete disclosure to everyone for whom you are acting and who is paying you anything. The safest course is to obtain the consent of all parties involved.

There was a case where an agent used information that he learned to acquire an interest in a property, without disclosing this information to his seller. The seller subsequently refused to pay the agent commission, which amounted to $10,000. The agent sued for the commission. The seller counterclaimed for the profit that the agent earned on the transaction personally. The judge awarded the agent his $10,000 commission.

The judge also awarded the seller $325,000 in the counter-claim. And of course the lawyers took their full fees from both sides. I have already given my opinion about starting litigation to recover your commissions. This was a great example where the agent was very misguided in starting these proceedings. All of it could probably have been avoided if the agent had just disclosed his interest in the first place. The seller would have most likely consented to the agent making a profit and the matter could easily have been resolved without litigation.

Don't deal with another agent's customers or do anything that attempts to affect the relationship between an agent and their existing customers. It may be tempting at times to deal with another agent's customers, especially when they approach you themselves wanting your services. Typically, this involves buyers who feel that they can save a few dollars by cutting out their own agent, hoping that you will reduce your listing commission if it appears that you will also be double ending the deal.

In the discipline proceeding involving Davis, decided April 17, 2001, the buyer agent acknowledged dealing directly with the seller's solicitor on a transaction, thereby avoiding the listing broker entirely. The agent was attempting to salvage the transaction, which had developed problems prior to closing as a result of concerns with the septic system on the property. The fine payable was $800 together with costs in the amount of $1,000.

Do not bad-mouth another agent in order to obtain a listing. I have heard of numerous situations in which agents have attempted to discredit another agent in front of that agent's clients in order to embarrass the agent and demonstrate their own special skills. All the agent accomplishes is to demonstrate how truly unprofessional he is, usually leaving an impression to all concerned of rude, arrogant behaviour. It is so important, in a business that is so dependent on word of mouth, that you do not damage your own brand image in this manner.

This also applies to how you treat people in your office. We all learn very early in our professional careers how dependent we become on the administrative staff in an organization. You need their assistance and support, especially when you get busy. Treating them with respect and courtesy at all times ensures that you will have their continued support, which will ultimately benefit your customers. This is called living your brand image or reputation in everything you do, every day.

When you are angry, the worst thing you can do is confront a person. You are most likely to say something that you will later regret. This is especially true of messages that you may leave on someone's voice mail when the person is not reachable. This voice mail can be used as evidence against you in a discipline or court proceeding. It reminds me of a kidnapping case in the mid-1980s when the kidnappers called from a motel that had caller ID, before many members of the public were aware what that technology was about. It took the police about five seconds to see where the call originated and apprehend the criminals.

In the discipline case of Imough, decided April 19, 2002, it was alleged that the agent had left messages with the buyers attempting to dissuade them from concluding their agreement of purchase and sale. The agent's defence was that it was a neighbour calling, who had wanted to disclose that the house being considered by the buyer had a leaky basement. As a result of these calls, the buyer withdrew from the property. The calls were traced back to the agent's office, through the applicable telephone records.

A RECO discipline proceeding is not a criminal trial, and therefore proof on a "balance of probabilities" is all that is needed. A tape of the telephone calls was played at the agent's hearing and a number of people involved stated that they recognized the voice as that of the agent. This behaviour was found to be "unjustified, unfair, and unprofessional." As a result of the seriousness of this violation, the agent had her licence suspended for three months and had to pay costs of $1,980.

One can assume that the cost to this agent was much more than three months' worth of commissions. It also involved a negative effect on her reputation, her relationship with other members of her real estate firm, and her relationship with other members of the profession.

A similar error is disparaging another agent in your written material or communications. In the discipline case of Hope, decided July 4, 2002, the agent issued a newsletter indicating that he was proud of being able to obtain the highest prices for properties in his area. He proceeded to disparage another agent in the newsletter, implying that the other agent only cared about closing the deal and not about doing the best service for his clients, including obtaining the highest price.

Although the other agent was not mentioned by name, it could easily be found based on the properties identified in the newsletter. It was held that Mr. Hope acted unprofessionally by disseminating negative and derogatory information about a fellow member. It was noted that as this happened in a relatively small community, the act of disparagement was very serious. The penalty in this case was $2,000 with costs of an additional $1,550.

In the case of Luzak, decided January 22, 2001, the agent advertised properties for sale even though the properties were under exclusive listing agreements with other brokers. This unauthorized advertising constituted unprofessional conduct, as well as a violation of the rules regarding advertising. The agent's position was that he was only advertising the properties as a potential buyer agent and that he could see nothing wrong with what he was doing. He further implied that these matters are not explained fully to most sellers who sign exclusive listings, and if sellers did understand, they would never have agreed to them.

On receiving complaints about these activities, the agent attempted to contact some of the sellers directly, to try to convince them that they had not truly understood what was meant by providing the listing agent with the sole authority to advertise that the property was for sale. This behaviour was further proof that the agent was attempting to interfere with the relationship between a listing agent and his client. The penalty in this case amounted to $6,000, with costs of $1,100.

In the discipline case of Woelk, decided February 4, 2002, the clients had a buyer agency agreement with a realtor. During the currency of this agreement, the buyers then contacted the agent about other properties. Woelk did not inquire whether there was another firm involved, nor did he try to contact the other realty firm, going on to sign the buyers to a different buyer agent agreement. The buyers subsequently purchased a property through his efforts. It was held that his action constituted unprofessional conduct in that he did not make any attempt to verify the existence of a second buyer agency relationship with the buyers, and failed to advise the buyers that they were potentially making themselves liable to pay two commissions on the same purchase, to each of the buyer agents noted in their two separate agreements. The penalty in this case was $750 and $250 in costs.

In the discipline case of Slavin, decided August 14, 2001, one agent attempted to take a listing from another agent, relying on the fact that the listing showed up for one day as having been cancelled on the MLS system. However, the mistake was corrected within 24 hours and could easily have been verified. Instead, the agent attempted to sign the seller to another listing agreement, exposing the seller to being bound by two separate agreements with two agents at the same time. It was irrelevant that the seller may have been unhappy with the first agent and wanted the listing to be cancelled. This was not sufficient justification for the second agent to try to take the listing.

The agent, on hearing that a complaint had been made by the first listing agent, left the following voice mail:

> I just got a call from the Real Estate Board saying that you've, ah, filed a complaint with them and RECO. Um, I think it is a shame that you did that, but ah, at the end of the day, um, over the next 12, 24, or 36 months, you will end up paying for this more than I will and ah, I will make sure, that ah, I keep an eye on everything you do from now on and in the future and I hope you don't break any rules and that you won't have any hassles from me. Always nice talking to you, take care, bye.

The agent was clearly upset after hearing about the complaint. It is only natural to become angry and want to yell at someone. Even if it was not intended to be threatening, the language used by the agent seemed to the committee to imply threatening behaviour. This entire tirade was viewed as unprofessional conduct. The fine levied was $3,000.

The worst thing you can do when a complaint is made against you is to say anything during this initial period that will only get you into more trouble later. The best thing is to cool down and discuss the situation with your own broker or legal advisers to determine the appropriate next step. It is well documented that what you do right after a complaint has been made can go a long way in determining the kind of remedy that will be sought by the investigating officer, whether it be mediation or a hearing. It does you no good whatsoever to attempt to throw your weight around. All this does is further confirm to any investigator that you commonly engage in unprofessional conduct.

Weisleder's Wisdom on . . . UNPROFESSIONAL CONDUCT

1. Always verify whether your client is under an agreement with another realtor. Get this confirmation in writing.

2. Never make disparaging remarks about other agents, whether in verbal conversations, voice mails, e-mails, documents, or newsletters.

3. Treat every agent, client, and administrative staff with courtesy and respect at all times.

4. If a complaint is made against you, resist the temptation to become angry at the person who made the complaint. Do not contact them when you are in this agitated state.

Broker Responsibility (Rule 43)

A broker shall be responsible for the professional conduct and professional actions of those Members registered with that broker.

Guiding Principle

43.1 This rule applies regardless of the legal relationship between the broker and the Member registered with that broker.

In the decision of Madsen, decided April 30, 2002, the agent was reported as having advertised the following: "Don't be misled. We pay 2.5% commissions to every selling broker." There were several listings where 2.5% was not paid by this broker. Rule 21 on misleading advertising had thus been violated. The agent paid a penalty of $1,200 and the broker paid $750 plus costs in the amount of $1,700.

The subject of misleading advertising is discussed in greater detail later in this chapter. The decision above was interesting in terms of the panel's views on broker responsibility for advertisements that bear the broker's name. The panel noted the following:

Since transactions are carried out in the broker's name and the Real Estate and Business Brokers Act mandates that any advertisement by a salesperson clearly identify the broker with whom the salesperson is registered, brokers should be *scrupulous* in ensuring that advertisements which are published are accurate and not misleading to the general public or to other RECO Members. Inaccurate, misleading advertisements do not only adversely affect the reputations of individual salespersons and brokers; they can also erode public confidence in the integrity of the real estate profession as a whole.

As you can see, the broker, for the general protection of the public, is held to an almost absolute liability standard when it comes to certain offences committed by the salespeople who work for them. For this reason, brokers must have proper guidelines in place as to how all advertising will be conducted. For example, they should ensure that the name of the broker is always equal to or larger than the name of the salesperson listed. Also, each real estate office should develop a process by which written approval must be obtained for all advertising that is intended for the public, whether it is to appear in newspapers, on radio or television, or even just in newsletters and flyers.

In the case of Ebrahim, decided January 9, 2002, already discussed in detail under Rule 1, Ethical Behaviour, the broker was also found to have been responsible for this agent's actions. In their defence, the broker indicated that they had no knowledge of any matters related to the transaction in question. No one had brought any concerns to the broker's attention, including the listing agent and all other parties in the transaction. The broker also brought in evidence that they held seminars for their salespersons regarding updates in the profession and had repeatedly advised each salesperson not to make any personal promises in a transaction, which was one of the key findings against the agent. The panel found that the broker did not provide adequate supervision and therefore was in breach of Rule 43. The panel concluded that

> given the mandatory language of Rule 43, given that the activities of the agent in the circumstances were being carried out in the name of the corporate broker, and given the evidence that the agent's conduct was unprofessional, liability for the broker arises under Rule 43. There is no stated requirement in Rule 43 that the broker with whom a salesperson is registered must have had knowledge or ought to have known of unprofessional conduct on the part of a salesperson before responsibility under this Rule 43 will arise.

Again we see that there is a standard of absolute liability that will be imposed in virtually all cases where an agent is found to have violated one of the rules. Not having knowledge of the behaviour is not accepted as an excuse. Many organizations have initial training programs for their new hires, beyond what is educationally required by the local real estate boards for membership. This includes ongoing supervision by senior agents in the office, especially in the first year of the junior agent's employment.

There are a number of positive benefits from taking this course of action. A broker that deploys its agents to act as mentors to other agents empowers its employees. The interest that they take in guiding less experienced salespeople will equally serve to reinforce these important principles in the entire brokerage. Such a broker is also creating loyal employees, and loyal employees are less likely to leave. It has long been demonstrated that those companies that have more loyal employees also have more loyal, and thus more profitable, customers. Engaging senior agents with junior ones reduces the risk of errors created by inexperienced agents that could result in liability under Rule 43. It also provides the added benefit of creating long-term loyal employees for your company that will no doubt lead to long-term loyal relationships with your customers.

Weisleder's Wisdom on . . . BROKER RESPONSIBILITY

---

1. Remember that real estate brokers will be held to a very strict standard of liability for all actions of their employee agents.

2. Be vigilant in all advertising conducted by members of your company. Ensure that proper guidelines and approval processes are set.

3. Have a proper orientation for new employees, including all policies, procedures, duties, and systems that they will be expected to learn.

4. Set up a proper supervision and mentoring program for new agents, to ensure that the work is performed to an appropriate standard.

5. Creating long-term loyal employees will lead to long-term loyal customers.

Competence (Rule 42)

A Member should render conscientious service with the knowledge, skill, judgment, and competence in conformity with this Code of Ethics and the standards which are reasonably expected of Members. When the Member is unable to render such a service, either alone or with the aid of another Member, the Member shall decline to act.

Guiding Principles
42.1 A Member should provide timely service to Clients and Customers and should respond appropriately to all communications with any participant to a Transaction.
42.2 When giving advice or an opinion, the Member should give

Clients a competent opinion based on knowledge of the relevant facts, an adequate consideration of the applicable law, and the Member's own experience and expertise.

42.3 A Member should only delegate or assign tasks to unregistered staff or assistants appropriate for an unregistered Person to perform.

42.4 A Member should not delegate or assign tasks to unregistered staff or assistants that constitute trading in Property including but not limited to being on site at an open house, door to door or telephone solicitation, showing Properties, or participating in an Offer or a listing presentation.

42.5 A Member should supervise the staff or assistants to whom the Member delegates or assigns a task sufficient to ensure that the task is performed appropriately. The supervising Member should be responsible for all services rendered and the Member should ensure that a registered Person retains the direct relationship with the Client. The tasks delegated or assigned to unregistered staff or assistants should be done under the direct supervision of the Member.

I remember when I first graduated as a lawyer and was called to the bar in Ontario. Under the terms of my membership with the Law Society of Upper Canada, I was immediately deemed to know every law and every statute and procedure that affected any potential client in Canada. This meant that the minute I decided to represent someone in any matter, whether it was a real estate transaction, a civil proceeding, or drafting a will, I was expected to immediately know everything that someone would know who had practised in a specific area for ten years. Talk about high — and unreasonable — expectations! I could never be expected to know everything — besides, everything wasn't covered in my textbooks at law school.

The fact is, most of what you do daily in the real estate

profession is not available in a textbook. You can only learn by practising. At the beginning of my career, every file that I worked on was supervised by a senior lawyer at my firm. I was also given precedent files so I could review all the forms that were involved in a typical transaction and read up on related issues that affected the transaction as well.

Most who are involved in the day-to-day real estate law practice will tell you that even after 20 years of being expert in one area of the law, they are still learning new things. It is generally recognized that you must continuously update yourself with education programs as the law is always changing and the way we practise continues to change. Who would have thought ten years ago that title transfers could be done with the push of a button from a computer in your office, in less than a minute, as compared with day-long lineups at the Registry office?

Even after I had developed an expertise in real estate transactions, I was still uncomfortable about handling a cottage property transaction, because I was not familiar with local issues. I remember doing a transaction and sending a letter to the Department of Health asking about the condition of the septic system at a cottage property. I received a letter in response telling me that I should contact the Ministry of Environment. So I sent a letter to that ministry and received a letter stating that I should be calling the Department of Health. Back to square one. I had no idea how to check the legality of the system. It was only through contact with local lawyers that I learned that in this particular town this fell under the jurisdiction of the local Building Department and that I should speak to a local inspector who was very knowledgeable about these issues.

Similar principles apply to real estate agencies. If you are not sure about something, ask for assistance. When you are relatively new in the business, never prepare an offer unless you have had it approved by a senior agent or the broker in your office who is acting in a supervisory role to you.

In the same way, do not assume that knowing how to do a certain type of transaction, such as a resale residential home in an urban area, automatically qualifies you to give advice on a cottage property purchase, a commercial property, or a condominium. Each area requires a certain expertise that only comes with experience. Recognize when you need assistance and do not be afraid to ask for help. It may take longer to get a transaction completed, or you may even be forced to give up a potential client, but in the end you will succeed in serving the clients you do take on in the most professional manner possible.

When we examine the errors that agents make under this rule, in many instances it is based on careless errors and is also often combined with Rule 11, failing to discover the proper facts in a transaction, or Rule 6, failing to draft the written agreement correctly. When you don't check out all the proper facts, by not listening to your client's needs, you will be in violation of your duty of competence. Your customer has the right to expect that when they tell you their needs and concerns, you not only will listen to them, but, more importantly, you will also find out anything that relates to their concerns and then protect them when drafting the written agreement.

The bar is raised as well when you are acting for a buyer, both in recommending the appropriate conditions to protect them and then writing those conditions correctly when completing the agreement. In Chapter 1, in the discussion of conditions and the case of Marshall, we saw just how important it was to accurately state all appropriate language in a condition, especially when representing a buyer.

The discipline case of Sawan, decided September 24, 2002, involved a number of instances where the standards displayed by the agent did not satisfy the duty of competence. There was a residential tenant on the property being sold. It was under-stood by all that there would have to be vacant possession granted on closing. The agent took it upon himself to prepare the notice to the tenant, in accordance with the applicable Tenant Protection legislation. The notice was given on September 15, 2001, which meant that the tenant did not have to vacate until November 15, 2001. Yet the agent said to the buyer that it would be no problem to move the closing up from October 31 to October 18, 2001.

Anyone who practises in the area of residential tenancies knows that there is virtually no guarantee that you can ever give concerning when a tenant will actually vacate a property, regardless of when a notice is given. A seller is much better off obtaining an agreement from the tenant in advance to vacate the property, rather than rely on any notice to terminate. In order to obtain the voluntary agreement of the tenant to vacate, you will have to provide some compensation to the tenant. However, this is far more preferable to going through the landlord and tenant court process. Most people do not realize that any notice to vacate given to a residential tenant states right on it that the tenant does not have to vacate the property on the date specified. The tenant has the right to dis-pute the reason for the notice, after which the landlord will have to commence proceedings to evict the tenant.

Tenants can be very clever in delaying these proceedings. Even if everything goes well, you still have to go through all the steps of serving the correct papers, obtaining a court date (which usually takes three to four weeks), attending a trial, obtaining and then entering the order, and possibly, in the end, even resorting to calling in the sheriff to forcibly evict the tenant. You can also expect counter-arguments from the ten-ants in these proceedings alleging all kinds of human rights abuses, failure to provide essential services, and of course, harassment — sometimes even sexual harassment.

There are also "professional tenants," experts in all areas of landlord and tenant law who know how to delay the process for up to six months. Even if all goes well, you are still looking at another 60 days from the date set out in your notice until the date you obtain vacant possession. Furthermore, if you have an uncooperative tenant, it will be difficult for you to conduct showings or open houses to even sell the property in the first place.

It is far more preferable, therefore, to obtain the voluntary agreement of the tenant in advance to vacate. This will lead to a more cooperative tenant when you show the property and provide no headaches when it comes time to deliver vacant possession on closing. Yes, it will cost the seller some money, maybe even two months' rent. But remember, the worst settlement is still much better than the best lawsuit. A typical landlord and tenant proceeding will take two to six months. You will waste at least one to two days in court and incur legal fees on top of that which will be nearly impossible to recover.

Had Mr. Sawan practised in this area of real estate, he would have realized not only that the tenant did not have to move out until November 15, 2001, but that there was a possibility that he could still be on the property until well into 2002 if the notice was disputed. Fortunately for him, he was able to obtain the agreement of the tenant to vacate prior to the October 31, 2001, closing date.

It would not be a valid defence to state that you are not an expert in tenancy law. If you take it on yourself to obtain vacant possession of a property, you will be deemed to know all the consequences.

As part of the preparation process, whether with buyers or sellers, the issue of residential tenancies may arise. Whenever a seller has the property rented to tenants, you must immediately review with the owner the obstacles that they may face if they want to give vacant possession of the property on closing.

Do not wait until an offer is signed to deal with what may be an uncooperative tenant. Do this right away, before a lot of time and money is invested in marketing the property for sale.

From a buyer standpoint, most first-time home buyers are currently renting an apartment. As the agent, you must therefore make inquiries as to what obligations they have under any lease commitment. Even if their lease is month to month, they will still have to provide the landlord with 60 days' notice prior to vacating their unit. You will want to ensure that you fix a closing date with this in mind, so that your clients are not paying additional rental costs on their current apartment after the transaction has been completed.

We discussed in Chapter 1 how conditions should be worded. In the Sawan case, the agent inserted a condition for the benefit of the buyers as follows:

> This offer is conditional upon the Buyer's solicitor reviewing the following condominium corporations documentation: Status Certificate, the last annual financial statements and finding all of the foregoing satisfactory to the buyer's solicitor sole and unfettered discretion.

The clause was partially satisfactory but failed to contain the consequences clause, that is, what happens if the solicitor is not satisfied? Can the buyer get out of the deal? As we saw in the Marshall case, judges view the actual language in a condition very strictly. It is easy to see how mistakes such as these can be made. How many agents make it a practice to just copy the clause or simply cut and paste clauses from their office precedents into agreements? Not taking the proper care in preparing your documents is how errors happen.

The failure of the agent to include this consequences language was found to be a violation of his duty of competence by the discipline committee. The agent also told the buyer and the seller that it would be "no problem" moving the closing date of the transaction from October 31 to October 18, but nothing was obtained in writing. It is clear that any important change to the agreement, such as a change in the closing date, must be made with a written amendment signed by both parties. The agent's actions were deemed to be a violation of Rule 1, and Rule 2 as well (the primary duty to clients).

Finally, there was a problem with the central vacuum system on the property. This system was not in operating condition on closing. The discipline committee found that the agreement should have contained language that at least stated that the chattels to be conveyed would be in good working order on closing.

Most sellers will not give warranties that survive closing. That is why they permit buyers to conduct home inspections, to satisfy themselves of the condition of the property and any chattels to be assumed on closing. However, most sellers will probably not object to a clause that states that these same chattels will be in good working order on the date of closing. The Sawan case indicates that this will be a minimum standard required of agents who act for buyers. If the clause is inserted and then removed by the seller, it can then be discussed with the buyer as to the consequences of its removal. Then the decision is the buyer's to make. However, by not inserting the clause in the first place, there is no proof that the issue was ever even discussed with the buyer. The penalty given for all violations in the Sawan case was $2,500 and $1,900 for costs.

The discipline case of Porteous, decided May 15, 2001, is a good example of what happens when you act for someone buying a property in an area where you are not familiar with many of the local issues. In this case, the agent acted as a buyer agent. He showed the buyers a property in an area where he had not practised before, based on a newspaper advertisement that the buyers had discovered themselves.

The agent told the buyers that in his opinion, home inspections were generally of no benefit because inspectors needed to give favourable reports. He would have recommended a contractor instead, he said. The point is that no home inspection was conducted prior to the offer being signed.

The agreement did provide that the seller would supply a well driller's certificate confirming that the flow of water on the property was at least three gallons per minute, and a certificate from the Ministry of Health confirming that the water was suitable for human consumption. The health certificate was obtained. Only one water test was conducted.

It turned out after closing that there was a problem with the drinking water. It was normal in this area to conduct at least three such tests on any well prior to closing any transactions, and was common knowledge for practitioners in the area. Proper tests were conducted by the buyer after closing, and it was found that the water was, in fact, unsafe for drinking.

It was also discovered after closing that nothing was filled in on the seller property information statement in the area asking, "Are you aware of any problem re quantity or quality of the well water?" This lack of disclosure was not conveyed by the agent to the buyer. In addition, there were many structural and mechanical problems with the house on the property that probably would have been discovered if an appropriate home inspection had been conducted.

Besides finding that Rule 1 on ethics, Rule 2 on duty to client, and Rule 11 on finding out facts were violated, the panel deemed there to have been a lack of competence. The agent should have investigated more thoroughly the suitability of this property to the buyer. A proper home inspection should have been conducted and more care should have been taken with the testing of the water. This is especially necessary since the Walkerton tragedy in Southern Ontario in the year 2000. I know many people in other parts of the country who refuse to drink municipal tap water to this day, even though there is nothing indicating any problems in most municipal water systems. The penalty for the agent was $5,000 plus costs of $1,600.

The competence rule also makes clear that agents should only assign tasks to unregistered staff that are appropriate for unregistered persons to perform. Some of the duties that should not be delegated include attendance at open houses, as well as preparation and/or presentation of offers and negotiations about offers. In the case of Cabral, decided January 11, 2001, the agent brought an unregistered assistant on an offer presentation. The agent indicated that the reason she brought the assistant was because she was concerned about security since she was visiting several properties that day. While the committee acknowledged that security was a valid reason, the unregistered agent should still not have been permitted to attend the offer presentation and to make comments during the negotiations. The fine in the case was $1,000.

Other activities that cross the line in this context include having an unlicenced employee do door-to-door or telephone solicitations, or show properties. It also includes giving them access to lock boxes that enable other registered agents to show a property when the listing agent is not available.

In the case of Amyotte, decided September 15, 2003, the agent used an unlicenced third party described as "part of the Amyotte team" to conduct a signback with the seller. Besides violating Rule 42, the agent was found by the panel to also be in violation of Rule 23, Obedience to Laws.

Weisleder's Wisdom on . . . COMPETENCE

1. You will always be held to the standard of an experienced realtor who practises in the field you are working in.
2. This standard encompasses not only areas of law that relate to your business, but local issues that may only be known by local realtors. Therefore, do not practise alone out of your own territory.
3. Do not permit unregistered agents to participate in any offer preparation, presentation, or negotiation.
4. If you are not sure about something, ask for assistance.
5. Do not give advice outside your area of expertise, such as landlord-tenant rights or whether a home inspection should be conducted.
6. Always listen to your client's instructions and follow through on any commitments you have made.

False Advertising (Rule 21)

A Member shall ensure that all advertising and promotion by or on behalf of the Member, including for Properties and services, is not false, misleading, or deceptive.

Guiding Principles

21.1 A Member may communicate factual, accurate, and verifiable information that a reasonable Person would consider relevant in the choice of a Member or in Buying or Selling Property.

21.2 A Member should not communicate information that is false, misleading, or deceptive, by the inclusion or omission of any information.

21.3 A Member should not use a Client's name or likeness, or the address of a Client's Property, in any advertising or promotional material, without the express written consent of the Client.

21.4 A Member should not advertise the price or terms of an Agreement about a Property that was bought or sold through the services of the Member without written consent from the Member's Client.

21.5 With respect to the use of the word "Specialist," a Member may only advertise as a "Commercial Specialist" or a "Residential Specialist" if a Member has satisfied the criteria established by the Council to be such a Specialist. Otherwise a Member may be put to the test of proving that any other term, title, or designation that implies that the Member is a Specialist or expert is not false, misleading, or deceptive advertising. A Member should not use a term, title, or designation restricted by the Council, unless the Member satisfies the criteria established by the Council for its use.

21.6 Sections 28 and 47 of the Real Estate and Business Brokers Act also apply to advertising.

Section 28 – Advertising

Every broker shall, when advertising to purchase, sell, exchange, or lease real estate, clearly indicate the broker's own name as being the party advertising and that he, she, or it is a broker, and any reference to the name of a salesperson in the advertisement shall clearly indicate the broker as being the employer of the salesperson.

Section 47 – False Advertising

Where the Registrar believes on reasonable and probable grounds that a broker is making false, misleading, or deceptive statements in any advertisement, circular, pamphlet, or similar material, the Registrar may order the immediate cessation of the use of such material and section 9 applies with necessary modifications to the order in the same manner as to a proposal by the registrar to refuse a registration and the order of the Registrar shall take effect immediately, but the Tribunal may grant a stay until the Registrar's order becomes final.

When we examine the Wheel of Misfortune for complaints made to RECO against real estate agents, the number one category is false advertising. In order to understand why agents are violating Rule 21, we need to understand what the rule means.

The law of false or misleading advertising in the private sector in Canada is governed by the Federal Competition Act, yet the principles under RECO are very similar to the ones that flow from this Federal legislation. The test used in any RECO hearing is the test that most judges use in any commercial dispute, asking, "How would a reasonable person in this situation interpret the advertising?" In the private sector, if the wording is written in a manner that is likely to deceive, substantial fines and penalties under the Competition Act may be invoked to serve as a deterrent and as a protection for the general public interest. The fact that these offences under the Competition Act carry significant civil fines and even criminal liability shows just how important this issue is to the federal government.

The test as to whether an advertisement in the real estate sector is misleading is not the meaning taken by the skilled and knowledgeable members of the public, but by the uninitiated and inexperienced who are exposed to it. In other words, what general impression does the advertisement leave? Let's look at some cases in which agents have faced difficulty under this rule.

In the case of Siu, decided August 7, 2003, a complaint was made against the agent by another agent. At issue were the agent's advertising activities. The particulars were as follows:

- The agent claimed in his advertisements, "We sell 1 house every 3 days";
- The broker name was considerably smaller than the agent's name; and
- The agent advertised properties sold by him without obtaining the written consent of the buyers.

When the committee looked at the facts surrounding the agent's sales records, it was clear that he did not sell one house every three days, in the literal meaning of the words. For this reason, he had violated Rule 21.

When a realtor commits a violation of this rule, there is usually a violation of Rule 1, Ethical Behaviour; Rule 10, Misrepresentation or Falsification; and Rule 46, Unprofessional Conduct. (Rule 46 can be looked at as a catch-all rule for any act that harms the interest of the public.)

The agent had to pay an administrative penalty of $3,000 as a result of this matter. His broker had to pay a $2,000 penalty as well, under Rule 43, in which the broker is held responsible for the professional actions of members registered with it. The broker was deemed to have permitted the agent to place the advertisements that were false and misleading, that displayed the agent's name in larger type than the broker's name, and that did not disclose the agent's correct status as a salesperson.

Showing a salesman's name in larger print than the broker's name in an advertisement is a common violation of Rule 21. It is worth noting the rather amusing situation involving Fulford, in a decision dated July 10, 2001. Mr. Fulford, an enterprising agent, rented a billboard in cottage country that displayed his name the same size as the broker's name. However, at night, the neon lights on the billboard displayed only the name of the agent, not the name of the broker.

In this case, the agent was required to repair the sign. A penalty was not awarded. I imagine the committee may have been slightly amused by his ingenuity. The agent had also been in constant contact with the RECO committee and had given his written undertaking to make the necessary changes to the sign shortly after being contacted about the problem.

In the case of Bird, decided April 15, 2003, the broker advertised that he was personally involved with 186 real estate transactions in 2001, or alternatively, that he "completed 222 transactions in 2001." It was later found that this was inaccurate because it also included sales by other salespersons who worked for the brokerage. Furthermore, this broker counted a sale twice if he acted for both the buyer and the seller. There was no qualifying language in the advertisements. The ad was found to be clearly misleading to the general public, in accordance with the general impression tests and principles noted above.

The issue of qualifying language brings up the discussion of typical disclaimers that are found on many advertisements, usually with an asterisk placed somewhere and then qualified in the fine print at the bottom. There are common sense principles associated with how we can use qualifying language. For example, the fine print cannot be used to distort the main meaning of the advertisement. It should not contradict the more prominent aspects of the advertisement and should be clearly visible. Consider an ad in which the words "Safe Beach" were asterisked to a note in the fine print that said, "Don't go in the water." Hey, don't laugh — it happens.

In the case of Mr. Siu noted above, it was found that he did not clearly set out his registration status as a salesperson in the advertisement. It was noted that "inconspicuous at the bottom left-hand corner (of the advertisement), in extremely fine print, were the words 'Harry Siu, Sales Representative.'" It is clear, then, that RECO does not consider inserting this kind of information into an advertisement by means of an asterisk as having complied with the code of ethics. Mr. Siu was found in violation of Rule 46, Unprofessional Conduct, as a result of this action. The broker was found in violation of Rule 43, Broker Responsibility, in permitting Mr. Siu to advertise in this way.

One of the ways the Bird case was resolved, besides the levying of an administrative penalty of $2,500, which Mr. Bird paid, was by receiving his agreement to use appropriate qualifying language in all his future advertisements. This language

was to be "in a typeface and in a sufficiently prominent position, as appropriate to the advertising medium, so that they
are clearly legible."

But he had also advertised that his clients saved "hundreds of
thousands of dollars by using his firm." This was based on the
fact that when his company acted on both sides of a transaction,
they only charged 3.5% commission, while the assumption is
that most sellers pay 6% for a similar listing commission with
other realtors. The 6% was deemed misleading because this was
not the uniform rate charged by most firms in this trading area
at the time. Furthermore, the advertisements were deemed not
to disclose sufficient information so that the reader could truly
understand the basis of the claim being made.

As part of the final decision, Mr. Bird also agreed that in
any future advertisement of this kind, he would clearly add in
accompanying language that "the claim is based on the difference between the actual commission rate clients were charged
and a hypothetical rate, as well as disclosure of the circumstances in which the actual rate was charged" (that it was in a
situation where they acted for both the buyer and the seller).
The statement also had to indicate that the hypothetical rate
used was not a universal rate charged by all brokers and that
commission rates are completely negotiable.

In addition, Mr. Bird agreed not to advertise any future
property being sold without the consent of the owner, following up on the principle from the Siu decision as well (and as
discussed in Chapter 4 on privacy legislation).

The reason for qualifying language is clear: To make sure
that the public understands the real basis of any claim that
you make and is not misled in any way.

I realize that in some of the advertisements I see in the
newspaper, the disclaimer language is so small that it is barely
readable or understandable. However, it usually will pass any

challenge under the Federal Competition Act. It seems clear from RECO's interpretation about the false advertising and misleading statement rules under the Code of Ethics that there may be a higher standard expected of real estate agents in this area, to ensure that the public interest is protected.

Many principles have been developed regarding comparison advertising, such as when a company attempts to claim that its products are better than its competitor's products. Due to the high profile nature of this type of advertising, and the negative effect it can have on the competitor's products, companies must be very careful to have the appropriate backup to prove what they say.

Suppose someone advertised the following:

> **I am the no. 1 agent in Canada***
>
> * In XYZ realty.

As you can see, the fine print drastically modifies the statement. If someone did not read the small print, they would adopt a much different impression.

This was so in the case of Katirai, decided November 12, 2002. Ms. Katirai had signs similar to the above advertised on a property that was for sale. Someone driving by would not have seen the modifying language on the sign, which identified the brokerage in small print.

The discipline committee thus concluded that the advertising was in fact misleading, in violation of Rule 21. The agent was fined $5,000. The broker was also found responsible for the agent's actions under Rule 43, and was fined $2,500. Furthermore, the agent was charged $1,400 for the costs of the proceedings, while the broker had to pay $700 toward costs.

In the discipline decision of Siu, dated October 24, 2001, the agent claimed in flyers that were distributed that he was the number one agent in total units and dollar value sold in North Scarborough during the past ten years. The committee looked at information obtained, which clearly indicated that another person was in fact the number one agent in total units and dollars sold in the area claimed by Mr. Siu in his advertising.

As the foregoing case illustrates, in order to make the claim that you are the number one agent, you must have the backup that proves the claim to the committee if challenged. For example, have you sold more homes than anyone else? Is the dollar value of all sales that you have done higher than anyone else? Did you earn the most real estate commissions in your area?

In the case of Boutette, decided October 30, 2003, the agent wrote the following on bench advertising: "Guelph's #1 Specialist." There was no qualifying language. The agent's name was also larger than the broker's and did not disclose the agent's status as a salesperson. Moreover, there was no evidence that the agent was a specialist. Besides violating Rule 21 on advertising, the case was found to be a violation of Rule 10, Misrepresentation; Rule 23, Obedience to Law; and Rule 46, Unprofessional Conduct. The fine was $1,000 to the principal of the brokerage and $3,000 to the brokerage itself, with costs of $1,000.

Consider this advertisement:

> **I have sold 10 homes within 5 days of listing, all at full price or more.**

This claim came under scrutiny in the Clarke case, decided June 20, 2002. On further examination, it was learned that some of the properties sold below full price, and the number of days until some of the properties sold had been understated as well. The penalty for the false advertising claim was $3,000 together with costs in the amount of $1,700.

Or take a look at this advertisement that came up in the case of Wallis-Simpson, decided July 31, 2002:

> **Guaranteed Sale Program.**
>
> **Move up to one of our homes and we will buy yours for cash.**

There were no other qualifiers in the ad. Not even the words "Terms and conditions apply," which are sometimes found in similar situations. The broker had printed a brochure about this guaranteed sales program. An examination of all the conditions applicable to this promotion made it clear that few buyers would in fact qualify for the program. None of these terms was referred to in the advertisement itself.

It's easy to give a guarantee. It is a lot harder to stand behind it. If you are going to advertise an unconditional guarantee, you had better be able to stand behind it or you will be the subject of a discipline or legal proceeding.

In the Wallis-Simpson example, the broker was found to be in violation of Rule 21 and was required to pay a penalty of $3,500 and $1,700 in costs.

In a case involving Wilson and Flat Fee Realty Inc., decided August 16, 2001, the following ad appeared:

WOW! Why Pay? 6% 5% 4% 3%
Full Service for Less with
Flat Fee Realty Inc.

The allegation in the case was that the advertising was misleading since it gave the impression that all fees would be less than 3% when in fact some fees were greater than 3% — and even greater than 6% under certain circumstances. The panel found that while the phrase "Full Service for Less" was not in itself misleading, it was so when combined with the declining commission percentages. The penalty was $500 against Wilson, $1,000 against Flat Fee Inc., and costs in the amount of $900.

Here's another claim to consider:

Top three Companies,
MLS Production Per Agent
MLS Statistics from January 1, 2000
till October 31, 2000

This advertisement was not placed in the newspaper but was used by the broker as a recruiting tool to attract new agents to their office. This broker did in fact have supporting evidence to make the claim and as a result, there was found to be no violation of the rule. The following statement from the decision is also interesting:

> There is always "boasting" by firms in advertising, whether it be real estate or otherwise. In this case, as there was no clear false statement, we cannot find Broker A in violation. However, RECO does take a dim view of any member that purposely produces advertising that misleads or confuses either the public or other parties and reminds members that they must be vigilant in ensuring the accuracy of their advertising.

This can probably be distinguished from the tongue-in-cheek, humorous advertising we are all familiar with. I have seen an ad by an agent who purports to have sold the Canadian Parliament buildings in Ottawa. Perhaps many members of the public wish it could be that easy to get rid of the government. It is doubtful that anyone would bring an action for false advertising against this agent. Most members would take the ad in the spirit in which it was written. Similarly, I have seen an agent with a Sold sign outside Casa Loma, one of Toronto's noted landmarks. Due to the fact that most people would not take this ad seriously, we can also say there was no attempt to deceive the public.

We will later review, under Rule 11, the results of failing to discover the correct facts, and how this alone can get agents acquainted with the Wheel of Misfortune. Sometimes factual situations under Rule 11 also catch Rule 21, when you enter information onto the local MLS system. For example, if you do not do your homework in finding out the actual dimensions of a property or the building located on it, or any features describing the property, you will invariably contravene Rule 21 when you try to advertise the property for sale, since you will be putting false advertising out to the public.

In the case of Swartz, decided June 14, 2002, the agent erred in collecting facts about the seller's property and advertised a building with 7,000 square feet when it only had 6,300 square feet. The facts, which were agreed to by both parties, were deemed to violate both Rule 11, Discovery of Facts, and Rule 21, False Advertising. The fine for the agent was $2,000, as well as costs of $1,500.

In a similar situation, involving Boyko, decided June 12, 2002, advertising contained information that the property was comprised of 2.75 acres, when in fact it was only 2.02 acres. Even though there was no intent to deceive anyone, the agent was found to have been careless in not verifying the information. The salesman made the argument that they should not be held responsible when they were relying on information told to them by the seller. However, we can see from the decision that responsibility is placed on an agent to try to find out important information, such as lot size, from other sources if the seller does not have sufficient information, *before* making any advertising claims. The penalty in this case was $4,000 and costs amounted to $1,700.

To assign liability under Rule 21, RECO does not have to prove that the agent or broker intended to deceive anyone. Even if the misleading statement is created inadvertently, the agent will still be held liable. In the case of Long, decided July 17, 2002, it was held that through inadvertence, the listing omitted information about an excluded third party offer. Even though there was a finding of fact that this was not intended by the agent, the agent still had to pay a relatively small fine, $250, but also had to pay the full costs of $1,700.

A similar situation can be found in the decision of Kurtz,

decided October 28, 2003. In this estate sale, the agent viewed the property personally to obtain the information for the MLS listing. He made an innocent error in describing that the house had aluminum siding when it really was wood. Although the panel found that this was the kind of error that could have been made by an agent of the "highest standards," it was still deemed to be a violation of Rule 21. If the agent was not 100% sure, then he should not have included this detail on a listing. Even though the error was not deemed malicious, it also unfortunately violated Rule 1 (2) about misrepresenting anything, as well as Rule 46 on unprofessional conduct. In the circumstances, there was no penalty awarded, but the agent was required to pay costs in the amount of $1,750.

Many will view this decision as being overly critical of the agent. Yet it does continue to illustrate the important principle of taking the time when you are gathering information from the seller to ensure that every fact contained in the MLS listing that will be viewed by the public is accurate and reliable. This will not remove any obligation of a buyer's agent to always be recommending a home inspection, but it does serve to protect the public interest by holding all agents to a higher standard when making this information available to the public.

Many real estate boards are now considering the practice of limiting situations in which brokers can insert the words "contact listing broker" in the remarks section of the listing. The intent is that all pertinent material information must be shown on the listing itself. All this reinforces your obligation to do what you can to get things right in the first place, when you are in the process of gathering information from your seller.

Regardless what your provincial code of ethics may say about advertising, these principles will remain the same. Since advertising by its nature is very public, and violations can have a negative effect on consumer perceptions toward the real estate profession in general, it's a small wonder that the majority of cases involving violations of codes of ethics have to do with violations of this rule on advertising. By following the principles set out in this chapter, you stand a great chance of never running afoul of the Wheel of Misfortune.

Weisleder's Wisdom on . . . FALSE ADVERTISING

1. Always have your advertising reviewed by your broker, or another agent in the office.
2. Ask yourself, "What impression am I creating with this advertisement? Is it likely to mislead anyone?" If you are not sure, get another opinion.
3. Make sure that the broker's name is at least as prominent as the agent's name.
4. Always specify your registration status in any advertisement, in a size that can be clearly recognized in the ad itself. Make sure your business cards also show the broker's name equally as prominent.
5. If you make any performance claim, make sure that you have the data to back it up.
6. Make no guarantees.
7. Make sure all your facts about a property are correct before you make any advertisements about the property.
8. If there is any qualifying language or disclaimer, make sure that it is large enough for anyone to see in the ordinary review of the advertisement, whether in a newspaper or flyer or on a billboard.
9. Assume that every advertisement may be reviewed by your local real estate association.
10. If the advertisement seems a little on the edge, ask yourself, "Is this worth a proceeding for the next eight months of my life, possible penalties, and a starring role on my association's Web site?" Then read the ad again.

Name (Rule 20)

A Member shall only practise using the Member's name as registered with the Council.

Guiding Principles

20.1 Where otherwise entitled to do so, a Member may practise with or through a business or corporate name so long as the Member's name as registered with or authorized by the Council accompanies each written use of the business or corporate name and Member's business card and letterhead contains the Member's name as well as the business or corporate name. However, the use of a business or corporate name is restricted by section 25 of the Real Estate and Business Brokers Act which is intended to prevent Members from creating the impression that the Member is practising with others when in fact the Member is practising alone.

20.2 A Member should not practise with or through a business or corporate name that could be confusing or misleading to the public.

20.3 A Member should ensure that the Member is introduced verbally to all participants to a Transaction by the Member's name as registered with or authorized by the Council at the earliest practical opportunity upon meeting or first speaking with the participants.

Section 25 – Carrying on business as individual

A broker carrying on business alone and not through an incorporated company shall carry on business in the broker's own name only and shall not use any description, words, or device that would indicate that the broker's business is being carried on by more than one person or by a company, but a surviving or remaining partner may carry on business in the name of the original partnership in which case the surviving or remaining partner shall publish on all letterheads and circulars used by the

*surviving or remaining partner in connection with the business
the fact that the surviving or remaining partner is the sole pro-
prietor thereof.*

In the case of Tatomir, decided January 20, 2003, Mr. Tatomir
registered Web site addresses containing his competitors'
names, with pointers on the Web site. As a result of the pointers, if a consumer attempted to find this Web site, they were
automatically routed to Mr. Tatomir's own Web site. Mr.
Tatomir claimed that he did nothing wrong by purchasing
these other Web site addresses as they were available and not
being used at the time.

The panel found that this behaviour constituted a violation
of Rule 20 in that Mr. Tatomir was not conducting business
under his registered name. It was also found to be a violation
of Rule 1 (2), Ethical Behaviour, which protects the public
from fraud, misrepresentation, or unethical practice in connection with real estate transactions. This was further found
to be a violation of Rule 46, Unprofessional Conduct, because
"most people would view this conduct as dishonourable and
unprofessional."

The law is currently being written regarding Web site
names and trademark violations in other commercial areas.
None of those decisions was referred to in Mr. Tatomir's case.
In the meantime, a very common sense rule of thumb is being
used: Is it likely that this practice could deceive the general
public? The answer was yes and the penalty against Mr.
Tatomir was $5,000.

In the similar case of Kewley, decided October 30, 2003, the
agent registered domain names that were similar to other brokers in the area such that if someone typed in the name of the
other brokers, they would be led to Mr. Kewley's Web site. The
penalty in this case was $4,000 and $1,350 in costs.

As stated in the section about Rule 1 on ethical behaviour,

your reputation is your brand image that you build during the course of your career. It is what leads to successful referrals as well as loyal customers who return to use your services in the future. As these cases demonstrate, you must do everything you can to make sure that no one else tries to trade or encroach onto the brand name that you or your company creates in your community. This happens when agents open companies with similar sounding names, or use any Web site manoeuvring to try to show connections to your own company. Be vigilant.

In the case of Dodds, decided April 3, 2002, the agent was found to have violated Rule 20 for carelessly carrying on business under the name of Jack Dodds when he was registered with RECO under the name of John Dodds. Although this seems a minor or technical violation, it serves to point out the importance of consistently using the name that you have filed with RECO, with no alterations.

RECO and the Ontario Real Estate Association take name registration very seriously. That is why they always take the position that the name that you use in identifying yourself to the public should be identical to the name that you have been registered under. Do not use any nicknames or call yourself part of anyone's team.

Weisleder's Wisdom on . . . NAME

1. Be vigilant in how your name is used in all correspondence, advertising, and signage; it must be consistent with the name that you are registered under.
2. Make sure that no one else is trying to use your name or any part of it in any manner that would create confusion in the public.
3. Do not attempt to use anyone else's registered name improperly, either through Internet links or other advertising.
4. If you discover a situation in which someone is trying to

use all or part of your name, act immediately with written correspondence, followed by legal action, if necessary, to protect your rights.

Discovery of Facts (Rule 11)

A Member shall discover and verify the pertinent facts relating to the Property and Transaction relevant to the Member's Client that a reasonably prudent Member would discover in order to fulfill the obligation to avoid error, misrepresentation, or concealment of pertinent facts.

Guiding Principles

11.1 Any fact that would affect a reasonable Person's decision to Sell the Property, the price for which a reasonable Person might be able to Sell the Property or a reasonable Person's ability to Sell the Property at a future date is a pertinent fact.

11.2 Any fact that could affect a reasonable Person's decision to Buy the Property, the price that a reasonable Person might pay for the Property or a reasonable Person's ability to resell the Property at a future date is a pertinent fact.

11.3 A Member representing a Seller of Residential Property should consider requiring that the Seller complete and sign a Seller Property Information Statement and should attach a copy to the Agreement or provide in the Agreement, or otherwise, in writing to the Parties, a statement that the Seller refused or was unable to complete the Statement.

11.4 A Member should not rely completely on the information obtained from the Client when such information is pertinent and it can be practicably verified from an independent source.

11.5 A Member representing the Seller should not recommend the acceptance of a condition where financing is being provided by the Seller without first recommending that the Seller verify the creditworthiness of the Purchaser.

11.6 A Member should, unless it is impractical to do so, verify pertinent facts and should not simply rely upon estimates or copies of information from previous sources.

11.7 Section 33 of the Real Estate and Business Brokers Act requires disclosure of financial information on a trade in a business.

In the decision of Polson and Bell, decided January 28, 2003, the seller told the listing agent that the property taxes were $5,300 and this amount was shown on the listing information. The sellers were not able to provide written confirmation. The listing agent did nothing further to verify the taxes. It turned out that they were in fact $6,248. The buyer agent also did not attempt to verify them, even after being advised that the taxes were approximate. It was found by the panel that both agents were thus in violation of Rule 11 in failing to discover pertinent facts relating to a property. The fines were $1,800 for each agent and the broker and $1,000 in costs for each party.

These kinds of errors are not made intentionally. There is no intent to deceive anyone. It is a case of simple carelessness in not verifying all important facts about a property.

In a similar decision regarding Sidofsky and Tsang, decided May 10, 2001, the parties recorded the taxes as $1,680.96 in the listing information when in fact this amount was only the interim tax bill. The actual taxes were $3,361.95. Not only were the agents found to have violated Rule 11, they were also deemed to have violated Rule 21 relating to false advertising. The penalties in this case were $200 each. All this could have been avoided if they were just a little more careful.

As often happens, violation of Rule 11 also brings about a violation of Rule 42, Competence, as well as Rule 2, Primary Duty to Client. In the decision of Bruno, decided February 13, 2003, the agent acted as a dual agent without obtaining a buyer agency agreement from the buyer. Although the buyer had expressed concerns about the water quality and recovery rate, no further actions were taken by the agent to verify these concerns or include a condition in the agreement to protect the buyer in this regard. The buyer later found out that the quality of the water was unsafe and that the recovery rate was inadequate.

Ms. Bruno was thus found to have breached Rule 11 about discovery of facts. Rule 42, Competence, and Rule 2, Primary Duty to Client, were also deemed violated. As there was no buyer agency agreement entered into, this was also deemed to be a violation of Rule 4, Written Representation Agreements. The penalty was $2,000 with costs of $1,750.

In the case of Verbakel, decided July 17, 2001, the agent erred in advertising that the house contained hardwood floors throughout. In fact, many rooms were unfinished. Most of the floors were under carpeting or area rugs. The agent stated that he relied on the Seller Property Information Statement filled in by the seller. However, the form was not clearly explained to the seller and the agent took no action to verify any of the statements made. This was deemed to violate Rule 11. This also resulted in a violation of Rule 21 against misleading advertising. The penalty was $750 and costs in the amount of $350.

The agent in the case of Karson, decided April 20, 2001, who was acting for both the seller and the buyer, indicated to the buyer that the property was a fully serviced lot. She relied solely on representations made by the seller, without doing any independent verification. The panel found this to be a violation of Rule 11 as well as Rule 2, Primary Duty to Client. The penalty was $500 with costs of $500.

In the section on competence (Rule 42) earlier in this chapter, I stressed that if you are not sure about a new region, you should beware of acting in it alone, because you will be held to the same standard as someone who has practised in that region for years. It makes no difference that you were doing your best and were not trying to deceive anyone. In the case of

Richie and Grime, decided November 30, 2001, the buyer agent, Ms. Grime, was not familiar with the region where the property was being purchased. Had she been from the community, she would have known that an adverse land designation had been passed affecting the property, which would probably have a detrimental financial effect on the property in the long term. The buyers indicated that they would never have signed the agreement in the first place had they known of this designation.

The panel found that Ms. Grime was honest, straightforward, and dedicated to her clients. Save for this lack of knowledge, she was also found to have otherwise acted as a good and prudent representative for her clients. Nevertheless, the panel found that she should have known about this designation and it was no excuse that she hadn't known about the land designation since she did not live there.

The listing agent, Mr. Richie, did know about the adverse designation and did not disclose this, and was thus found in violation of Rule 1 on dealing fairly, honestly, and with integrity with the public, other members, and third parties. The penalty for Ms. Grime was $1,000 and $300 in costs. The penalty for Mr. Richie was $3,000 and $900 in costs.

In a similar case of Woodley, Irwin, and Rolph, decided October 23, 2003, the seller had completed a Seller Property Information Statement, which indicated that the lands were zoned as "hazard land," meaning that there were limits as to what could be built on the property. This fact was left out of the listing information. The SPIS statement was not requested by the buyer agent. The buyer agent was deemed to have violated Rule 11 for not checking the seller's property information statement as well as not knowing about the hazard lands situation that affected many properties in this area. In failing to disclose this on the listing information sheet, the listing agent was also deemed to have violated Rule 10 on misrepresentation as well as Rule 46 on unprofessional conduct. The fines were $5,500 for the listing and buyer agents and $1,500 in costs.

As I have indicated, when you violate the principles of the Code of Ethics, you may also put yourself in a position where legal proceedings are brought against you. Most legal cases are framed in negligence, whereby the agent has fallen short of the standard expected of him, either through commission of an act or omission. Besides violating the concept of full disclosure, which is usually one of the significant factors in any legal claim, the three code of ethics rules that are commonly associated with a legal claim based in negligence are Competence (Rule 42), Discovery of Facts (Rule 11), and Misrepresentation (Rule 10). When an agent fails in following these rules, he will also leave himself open to a potential legal claim for negligence.

In the legal decision of Winsham, decided April 20, 2001, a listing agent had described a property as having 46,600 square feet. The marketing package that accompanied the document attempted to include a disclaimer that the agent could not guarantee the accuracy of the document itself. The buyer expressed some concerns about the square footage but was advised by the buyer agent that the buyer could be protected with a clause in the agreement. No clause was included as the buyer relied on representations by both the buyer agent and the listing agent. It turned out that the property was only 44,697 square feet.

In this case the listing agent was careless in that the documents in the seller's possession also indicated the discrepancy in the square footage. The buyer agent did not do enough to protect the buyer with a clause in the agreement and/or suggest to the buyer that he retain a surveyor or other expert to assist in the determination of the square footage if it was important to him.

The judge ruled that both the listing and the selling agents were partially responsible and had to contribute to the damage award. The buyer was also held to be partially responsible as he was deemed to be somewhat of an expert in these kinds of purchases and could have taken steps on his own to protect himself.

While the seller's agent was simply not careful in reviewing the documents that he had in his possession, the buyer agent did not listen to his customer's concerns. If he had, he would have known that the square footage was important to the buyer and could have protected the buyer either with an appropriate condition or by obtaining an up-to-date survey of the property. Had both agents just taken the time to make certain that the facts about the square footage were carefully discovered, this entire legal proceeding could have been avoided.

Weisleder's Wisdom on . . . DISCOVERY OF FACTS

1. Be very careful when checking all facts relating to a transaction.
2. Verify anything told to you by your client with written information or by proper visual inspection, where possible.
3. If information cannot be verified, disclose this as early as possible to your client so that they can make any required informed decision.
4. If a Seller Property Information Statement is available to a buyer agent, make sure you review it carefully with your client.
5. After determining your buyer client's needs, be careful in following up all facts necessary to satisfy your client's requirements.

Misrepresentation or Falsification (Rule 10)
A Member shall not make any statement or participate in the creation of any document or statement that the Member knows or ought to know is false or misleading.

Guiding Principles
10.1 A Member should be honest and candid when advising Clients.
10.2 A Member should not participate in any arrangement to conceal or withhold any facts pertaining to a Property.

When an agent is in violation of Rule 10, you can bet that there are legal proceedings taking place at the same time. Any violation of this rule virtually also guarantees that the agent has violated Rule 1, Ethical Behaviour, as well as Rule 46, Unprofessional Conduct. When I look at the cases that have dealt with this issue, I can only wonder, "What were these agents thinking?" However, it is easy to criticize someone after the fact, with the benefit of hindsight, without understanding the individual or business pressures that the agent may have been under at the time, whether in their personal lives, from their broker who expects them to deliver transactions, or from clients who want to get the deal done.

The moral of many of these cases is that it is never worth it, regardless of the pressure that you may be under. When you falsify a document, or conceal a material fact that will affect a transaction, you are just begging for your licence to be suspended or revoked. You are also leaving yourself open to legal proceedings. As indicated under the discussion about insurance in Chapter 2, there is an exclusion under the errors and omissions policy for fraudulent behaviour. Accordingly, not only may this type of behaviour lead to legal proceedings being brought against you, but the financial costs may be prohibitive to you or your broker if the insurer denies coverage in the circumstances.

In the discipline case involving Sharma, decided May 4, 2001, the agent had advertised that buyers could purchase a property with as little as 5% down and that there was a possibility that they could also get 3% of the deposit refunded as well. A buyer who responded to the ad was advised by the agent to see if they could initially qualify for a mortgage. As the buyer was only a temporary employee, Sharma advised them that they would not qualify for a mortgage.

Sharma offered to prepare a false employment letter to assist the buyer and asked for a $300 fee to obtain this letter. The letter that was prepared showed an annual full-time salary of $40,000 and indicated that the buyer was a "valuable asset of the company." The buyer subsequently entered into an agreement of purchase and sale and was able to obtain 90% financing on the basis of the letter. You guessed it: The buyer could not come up with the additional 10% and the transaction was aborted, with the buyer losing their $3,000 deposit. At the hearing, Sharma filed an undertaking to provide restitution to the buyer.

Given the serious nature of the matter, Sharma was fined $12,000 plus costs of $900, ordered to attend a RECO Code of Ethics course, and placed on probation for the maximum two years.

In the discipline case of Ebrahim, decided March 14, 2003, the agent prepared a gift letter to attempt to deceive a financial institution into thinking that the buyers had the sufficient down payment out of their own resources to complete the transaction. The gift letter appeared to be on a standard form document prepared by the agent, implying that this tactic may have been used by the agent in the past in other similar transactions. A false employment letter was prepared, showing a false company and a false annual income of $72,500, though there was no direct evidence that this letter was prepared by the agent. The transaction was ultimately aborted for a list of related reasons, given that the buyers did not have the resources to complete the transaction.

The agent did not attend the hearing. The preparation of the false gift letter was deemed an obvious violation of Rule

10. There was also deemed to be a serious violation of Rule 46, Unprofessional Conduct, and Rule 1 (2), Ethical Behaviour, in not protecting the public from fraud, misrepresentation, or unethical practice. Given that there was also a prior serious conviction against this agent, the penalty granted was probably the most extreme possible, a $25,000 fine, $1,750 in costs, plus the matter was referred to the Registrar for removal of the agent's licence.

In the discipline case of Mugford, decided October 22, 2001, an offer was prepared with a Schedule A that provided a rebate to the buyer of $2,500, purportedly for "legal fees and other closing costs." In fact, this was done to artificially raise the purchase price due to the fact that the buyers were in financial difficulty. The financial institutions were never provided with Schedule A. The agent also tried to get the buyers to falsify the dates on a waiver related to the home inspection condition. Further, the agent gave money to the buyer in order to artificially show a higher bank balance, as proof of their financial stability. The penalty levied was $7,500 with costs of $1,500, a three-month suspension, and a two-year probation.

In the case of Edgecombe, Mainella, Vass, and Azan, dated April 12, 2001, an initial agreement of Purchase and Sale was prepared between the seller and buyer for the sum of $178,000. A second agreement was then prepared between the same parties for the sum of $186,000, but the offer also contained an amendment that showed a credit of $8,000 to the buyer as a result of the fridge, stove, and broadloom not being included in the transaction. It appeared to the tribunal that the entire second offer was created to enable the buyer to obtain higher ratio financing.

What was interesting in this decision is that it was the bank, which had turned down the application for financing, that complained to RECO about this matter. The decision was also interesting in that it showed what can occur when inexperienced salespeople work on a transaction without the proper super-vision. All of the defendants had to pay penalties ranging from $2,500 to $5,000 and were placed on probation, demonstrating the seriousness of these events.

In the discipline decision of Lesky, decided October 17, 2001, a property listed by Mr. Lesky attracted no offers when it was listed at $99,000. For no apparent reason, the listing price was raised to $115,900 and accepted by buyers introduced to the property by a buyer agent. There was also a direction that was separate from the offer in which the seller agreed to pay back certain funds to the buyer.

The transaction was conditional on the buyers obtaining 85% financing. Lesky forged a waiver signed by the buyers, waiving the financing condition. This was done to assist the seller in arranging for mortgage financing for a new property that they wanted to purchase. Lesky stated that he did this under pressure from the seller, who needed this to obtain the desired financing. The seller denied everything.

The panel found that Lesky did not act alone in falsifying the waiver and was duped by an unscrupulous client. This client also agreed to pay the buyers back the sum of $18,000, which effectively reduced the actual purchase price to $95,000. The bank became suspicious of the transaction and the end result was that the buyers became tenants of the property.

Mr. Lesky attended the hearing and expressed remorse for his actions. The penalty against him was $5,000, with costs of $1,250, and his licence was suspended for a period of six months. It is not difficult to see that there were other unscrupulous parties in this transaction, including both the seller and the buyers, who were participating in transactions to artificially inflate the purchase price to obtain sufficient mortgage monies. But this is not a defence for any agent.

If you do your homework, it should not take long for you to

see the true colours of a particular seller, right at the listing presentation. Find out the financial situation of the property immediately, to see if the seller is over-mortgaged and in need of an immediate sale. Have the SPIS form filled out, so you can determine whether the seller has any issues with disclosure of important matters related to the property. Above all, the minute your client asks you to do anything that causes ethical bells to ring, get out of the relationship.

Unscrupulous clients know all the tricks. They are like professional shoppers. These people feel that if they can bother a salesman five times and take up hours of their time, the salesman will give them a better deal because they have already invested so much time with the buyer. Unscrupulous clients will try the same tactics. They will have you spend a tremendous amount of time with them before they start with the unethical suggestions, hoping that you will feel the same way — that you have invested too much time with them to walk away.

When you are faced with unscrupulous clients in your practice, think about the agents in these examples and the tragic results of their actions. Think about your licence to practise flying out the window. Think about the emotional and financial distress associated with RECO and possible legal proceedings. Then just say no.

In the discipline case involving Kiriakopoulos, decided May 1, 2001, the agent forged the signature of a seller to transfer a listing from the former broker's office where the agent worked to the new broker's office that employed the agent. The new broker terminated the agent's employment when he learned of the forgery. Not only was this behaviour deemed a violation of Rule 10, it was also deemed to violate Rule 46, Unprofessional Conduct, as well as Rule 1, Ethical Behaviour. The penalty was $15,000, with costs of $1,300, and the agent was placed on probation for two years.

In the case of Barrow, decided October 2, 2001, the agent

was a listing agent. The offer contained representations about the water well system and the septic system, two hot spots when dealing with these types of properties. In the course of dealings on this transaction, the parties agreed to retain a company to pump out the septic system, which was done. The invoice prepared by the company, which was given to the seller's agent, contained a recommendation that the system needed "baffle repair and bed treatment." The agent removed this recommendation from the invoice and the buyer only found out about this after the deal had closed.

The agent's position was that since repairs might be needed in the future, this was not pertinent information relating to the property. The panel disagreed, finding that this action by Barrow amounted to a violation of Rule 10 as well as Rule 46, Unprofessional Conduct. During the course of the hearing, there were other allegations made against the agent about further duties owed to the buyers regarding the well and the septic system that were not proven. Accordingly, the penalty given was a reprimand, with costs of $600.

Weisleder's Wisdom on . . .
MISREPRESENTATION OR FALSIFICATION

1. Do not participate in any way with any forged or altered document or in any scheme to artificially inflate the value of a property.

2. Do not agree to witness any signature if you are not present at the time.

3. Be wary of any document prepared outside the scope of the written offer to purchase that changes the purchase price or any other material term of the agreement.

4. Do not let yourself be used or tricked by an unscrupulous client, even if it means walking away from a possible commission.

Written Representation Agreements (Rule 4)

A Member shall enter into a written Representation Agreement with a Client at the earliest practical opportunity, and in all cases before any Offer to Purchase is submitted.

Guiding Principles

4.1 A Representation Agreement should specify the role and nature of services offered by the Member, the duration of the Agreement, the compensation of the Member, and the expectations and obligations of the Member and the Client.

4.2 A Member should put any representation or promises in writing including a representation or promise to permit the early cancellation of a listing or a representation agreement or a representation or promise to rebate or reduce a commission in some circumstances. Section 24 of the Real Estate and Business Brokers Act has special requirements about representations or promises to resell any real estate, Purchase or Sell real estate, to obtain a mortgage, lease or loan, and some similar Transactions.

4.3 A Representation Agreement should not be for a period of more than 6 months unless the Client specifically gives an Informed Consent to a longer period in writing and initials that provision.

4.4 The requirements of this Rule are in addition to the requirements in Rule 3 [Disclosure of Role].

4.5 Section 35 of the Real Estate and Business Brokers Act has specific provisions regarding Listing Agreements.

Section 24 – Promise to resell prohibited

24. No broker or salesperson shall, as an inducement to purchase, sell, or exchange real estate, make any representation or promise that the broker or salesperson or any other person will,

(a) resell or in any way guarantee or promise to resell any real estate offered for sale by the broker, the salesperson, or the other person;

(b) purchase or sell any of the buyer's real estate;

(c) procure a mortgage, extension of a mortgage, lease, or extension of a lease; or

(d) purchase or sell a mortgage or procure a loan, unless at the time of making the representation or promise the broker or salesperson making it delivers to the person to whom the representation or promise is made a statement signed by the broker or salesperson clearly setting forth all the details of the representation or promise made.

Section 35 – Agreement to list real estate with broker
35. (1) Every broker and salesperson shall, immediately after the execution of an agreement to list real estate for sale, exchange, lease, or rent with the broker, deliver to the person who has signed the agreement a true copy thereof.

Expiry of Agreement:
(2) An agreement with a broker to list real estate for sale, exchange, lease, or rent is not valid,

(a) if it does not contain a provision that it will expire on a certain date specified therein;

(b) if it contains more than one date on which it may expire; or

(c) if a true copy of it is not delivered by the broker or the broker's salesperson to the other party immediately after its execution.

In the discipline decision of Othmeier, decided November 1, 2002, the agent was purporting to do a favour for a friend. Because she did not intend to charge for her services, she did not prepare the usual representation agreements. The seller and buyer were introduced to each other by the agent, but the agent signed no representation agreement with either the seller or the buyer. She did assist in preparing the offer, with both the buyer and seller attending at her office, and proceeded to explain the terms of the offer to the buyer.

The agreement contained clauses that were deemed to be unclear and ambiguous, causing concerns in their interpretation. The panel found that her actions constituted a violation of Rule 4, in failing to document the agency relationships with both the seller and the buyer. She was also found in violation of the duty of competence as she failed to add appropriate terms, conditions, and obligations into the agreement itself. The penalty was $1,500, with costs of $2,200.

The panel was quite clear in its findings that it made no difference that the agent was not receiving any compensation. The proper course of conduct would have been to refer the clients to other agents and to refer them to a lawyer to draft any agreement. The lesson here is obvious. Even if you are acting for free on a transaction, you will be held to the same standards as if you were being paid in full. You can see that you are in fact doing yourself no favours when you act in this way for clients.

Doing favours may be the best way, in fact, to lose your friends. The same can be said when you act for relatives for no pay. It is probably the best way to upset your friends or develop unnecessary animosity from your relatives. You may think it is a favour, but they will still expect your best, so if you are not prepared to give your best, do not get involved.

Weisleder's Wisdom on . . .
WRITTEN REPRESENTATION AGREEMENTS

1. Avoid doing favours such as working for no remuneration. It inevitably leads to your not taking the same care in fulfilling your obligations.

2. If you are doing a favour, with no remuneration, remember that your standard of care must be exactly the same as if you were being paid in full.

Written Transaction Agreements (Rule 6)

A Member shall ensure that Agreements regarding Transactions are in writing, expressing specific terms, conditions, obligations, and commitments of the Parties to the Agreements and that copies of each accepted Agreement shall be furnished to each Party upon its final acceptance.

Guiding Principles

6.1 An accepted Agreement includes amendments, waivers, and other related documents.

6.2 A Member should make reasonable efforts to forward a copy of an accepted Agreement to a lawyer of a Party or a lender to a Party on the instructions of the Party and should notify the Parties promptly if the Member was unable to do so.

6.3 Sections 32 and 36 of the Real Estate and Business Brokers Act also apply here.

Section 32 – Breaking of contract prohibited

32. (1) No broker or salesperson shall induce any party to a contract for sale or rental of real estate to break the contract for the purpose of entering into another such contract.

(2) Unless agreed to in writing by the seller, no broker is entitled to claim commission from the seller in respect of a trade in real estate if the real estate is to the knowledge of the broker covered by an unexpired listing agreement with another broker.

(3) Every person signing a listing agreement or an agreement for sale or rental of real estate shall state with the person's signature the date upon which the signature was actually affixed.

Section 36 – Agreements to sell, purchase

36. Where a broker or salesperson has secured an acceptance of an offer to sell, purchase, exchange, lease, or rent real estate, the broker or salesperson shall require each of the parties to sign a sufficient number of copies of the agreement and the

broker or salesperson shall retain one signed copy and shall
forthwith deliver one signed copy to each of the parties.

In the discipline decision of Wong, decided October 21, 2003, the agent was representing an estate. As the listing price was not generating any offers, the agent reduced the listing price on the MLS. The agent claimed that he received verbal instructions from the seller, although the seller denied this. In any event, the panel found that under Rule 6, any change to the listing agreement had to have been completed in writing. This was also deemed to be a violation of ethical behaviour (Rule 1), Primary Duty to Client (Rule 2), and Unprofessional Conduct (Rule 46). The penalty awarded was $2,750, with costs of $1,350.

In the case of Demosani and Paget, decided April 26, 2001, there was confusion in the offer preparation regarding whether the appliances were to be included in the purchase price. The seller wanted them excluded and the buyer wanted them included. The evidence of both agents was that in the final agreement, the appliances were to be included but the agent did not include this in the agreement through error. The seller did not agree to leave the appliances.

The panel found that this error constituted a violation of Rule 6 in the failure to include this agreed upon term in the final written agreement. It was also held to be a violation of Rule 2, Primary Duty to Client; Rule 46, Unprofessional Conduct; and Rule 1, Ethical Behaviour. The buyer agent was given a penalty of $1,000 and the listing agent a penalty of $500. Both paid costs of $600.

In the case of Amyotte, decided September 15, 2003, the agent permitted the seller to accept an agreement of purchase and sale even though the seller disagreed that the pool and the dishwasher should not be included in the purchase price. The agent said it was no problem and that she would obtain the agreement of the buyers to delete the items in an amendment.

The buyers never agreed to the amendment. This was found to be a violation of Rule 6 as well as Rule 2, Primary Duty to Client. The penalty was $4,000 with costs of $1,000.

In the case of Carnell, dated January 28, 2004, the agreement of purchase and sale had been faxed so many times during the offer and acceptance process that it was virtually illegible, yet the agent permitted it to be signed by the parties. This was found to be a violation of Rule 6 and the fine was $3,000 with costs of $750.

When people ask me what qualities an organization looks for in new employees, I mention the obvious ones such as being hard working, dedicated, loyal, innovative, and friendly. But another big one, in my opinion, is being careful in everything you do. If you take care in filling out the minor points, the larger issues will take care of themselves. Once you develop good habits of being careful in everything that you do, you will find yourself better organized and less stressed, and will be working with a large number of very satisfied customers.

Weisleder's Wisdom on . . . WRITTEN TRANSACTION AGREEMENTS

1. Make sure that everything you do is put into writing as soon as possible.
2. All changes to written documents should also be reduced to writing.
3. Do not use offers after they have been faxed too many times and are for the most part illegible.
4. Take great care in filling out all sections of the agreement of purchase and sale, including all areas in the printed provisions and any schedules.

Financial Disclosure (Rule 5)

A Member shall disclose the financial aspects of a Transaction and any personal interest of a Member in a matter to the Parties sufficient to enable them to make an informed decision.

Guiding Principles
Disclosure of Expenses:
5.1 A Member should, prior to the signing of any agreement, fully inform the Client or Customer regarding the type of expenses, without necessarily specifying their nature for which the Person may normally be liable.
5.2 A Member should not suggest or imply, directly or indirectly, that the fees or commissions payable are set, fixed, or mandated by a real estate board or the Council.
5.3 A Member shall ensure, before incurring an obligation on behalf of a Client, that the Person providing the services or products knows who is responsible for payment.

Disclosure of Benefits:
5.4 A Member should disclose in writing to a Client or Customer, and obtain prior and Informed Consent in writing for: (a) any direct or indirect financial benefit or commission, rebate or fee that the Member or the Member's firm or a Related Party may receive from another Person other than the Client by virtue of the Member's services, including advice, recommendations, and referrals, (b) the approximate amount of such benefit, commission, rebate, or fee, and (c) the identity of the Person conferring the financial benefit, commission, rebate, or fee and the nature of the Member's relationship with that Person. However, where the financial benefit is a fee conferred from one broker to another broker, whether in Ontario or outside of Ontario, the consent need not be in writing.
5.5 A Member should not recommend or suggest to a Client or Customer the use of services or Products of another Person in

which the Member or a Related Person has a direct or indirect interest without disclosing such interest in writing at the time of the recommendation or suggestion. "Services or products" include lending institutions, solicitors, appraisers, insurers, moving companies but should not include other real estate brokerage firms.

5.6 A Member should, when requested, render a proper accounting to a Client with respect to money, Property, or other things which have been entrusted to the care of the Member.

5.7 A Member should disclose to the Member's Client all compensation the Member will receive by virtue of the Member's services. The phrase "by virtue of the Member's services" includes any benefit that may result from the Transaction itself.

Self Dealing:

5.8 A Member should not present an Offer or acquire an interest in Property either directly or indirectly for the Member or a Related Party without first delivering the Member's position to the Seller in writing. A Member should not Sell Property in which the Member or a Related Person has an interest without disclosing the Member's position to the Buyer in writing and obtaining an acknowledgement in writing. Section 31 of the Real Estate and Business Brokers Act applies to this situation.

5.9 In general, the Code of Ethics applies to a Member who acts as a principal in a Transaction or who represents a Related Person.

Application of Rule:

5.10 This rule applies to contemplated interests by a Member or a Related Person as well as interests in Property.

5.11 The disclosure in this Rule should be made at the earliest practical opportunity in the Transaction.

Section 31 – Statement where broker or salesperson purchases for resale

31. (1) No broker or salesperson shall purchase, lease, exchange, or otherwise acquire for himself, herself, or itself or make an offer to purchase, lease, exchange, or otherwise acquire for himself, herself, or itself either directly or indirectly, any interest in real estate for the purpose of resale unless the broker or salesperson first delivers to the seller a written statement that he, she, or it is a broker or salesperson, as the case may be, and the seller has acknowledged in writing that the seller has received the statement.

(2) Where real estate in respect of which a broker or salesperson is required to give a statement under subsection (1) is listed with any broker or, in the case of a salesperson, is listed with the broker by whom the salesperson is employed, appointed, or authorized to trade in real estate, the statement shall include,

(a) full disclosure of all facts within the broker's or salesperson's special knowledge that affect or will affect the resale value of the real estate; and

(b) the particulars of any negotiation or agreement by or on behalf of the broker or salesperson for the sale, exchange, lease, or other disposition of any interest in the real estate to any other person.

Throughout this book I have advised on the principle of full disclosure in everything that you do. This is what Rule 5 and Section 31 of the Real Estate and Business Brokers Act (REBBA) are all about. Disclose everything, especially any personal interest that you may have in any transaction, or if you are in fact purchasing a property yourself from either a seller who is not your client or a seller who is your client.

When an agent represents a client or customer in any transaction, they can provide many types of services besides the common listing and buyer agency services. The agent may assist the buyer in obtaining financing, or having an appraisal done on the property. They may assist the buyer in obtaining insurance for the property. These other services could result in the agent's receiving a fee from a third party, which we could refer to as an additional profit that the agent is making for providing the services to a seller or buyer. There is nothing wrong in principle with making this kind of profit, provided that you disclose everything in advance and obtain the approval of your client.

In the case of Norm Macdonald and James Macdonald, decided December 18, 2001, representations were made to the buyers that Norm was the owner of a property. Norm and James were brothers and were also registered brokers working together on this transaction. Although the seller was shown as A Inc., the buyers were led to believe that Norm was the owner of this company. The buyers then began dealing directly with the party who was the actual builder of the new home on the property, as though he was the owner. The buyers gave the seller an additional $20,000 to complete the property, and the money was taken and not accounted for. They had also paid over $15,000 in deposits. Many construction liens started piling up on the property, as the trades were also not paid by A Inc.

In fact, Norm was one of the owners of the property itself and had planned to transfer the property to the buyers directly, after the new home was built. Although A Inc. would build the house, and would be paid by the buyers, the title would transfer directly to the buyers from Norm.

It was found by the panel that Norm did not go far enough to explain his financial interest in the property itself. The buyers were under the mistaken impression that Norm did have an interest in the company owned by the builder and this was a factor in the buyers deciding to advance the extra funds directly to the builder in order to finish the house. Accordingly, Norm and James were found to have violated this rule on financial disclosure and the penalty was $1,000, with costs of $300. They were also held to violate Rule 6, regarding written agreements, as well as Rule 46, Unprofessional Conduct.

For the protection of the public interest, Section 31 of REBBA, noted above, makes it clear that a seller who is also a realtor makes full disclosure of this fact to any buyer. What this rule and this case further clarifies is that all details of any ownership, including any arrangements with third-party builders that may be permitted onto the property, must also be carefully documented to any potential buyer.

Weisleder's Wisdom on . . . FINANCIAL DISCLOSURE

1. Always disclose, in a detailed manner, any interest that you may have in any property or in any aspect of a transaction.
2. Ensure that all financial disclosure is given in writing.

Confidentiality (Rule 8)

A Member shall not disclose confidential information about the Client except with the Informed Consent of the Client or as required or authorized by law. The duty of confidentiality contin- ues after the professional relationship with the client has ended. A Member may disclose information without consent in order to prevent or assist authorities to prevent, investigate, or prosecute an offence, to defend a Member against an allegation by the Client of negligence or improper conduct.

Guiding Principles

8.1 Confidential Information includes information about a Client's assets, liabilities, income, personal expenses, motiva- tions to Buy or Sell, and previous Offers whether or not part of a public record.

8.2 A Member should not disclose or use confidential informa- tion for the Member's advantage or the advantage of a third party without the Client's consent.

8.3 A Member should ensure that a Client's consent to disclose

*or use confidential information is specific, is an Informed
Consent, and is made after full disclosure by the Member of the
nature of the proposed disclosure of information or the use to
which the information will be put.*

In Chapter 4, on privacy, I will discuss the need to protect all personal information in your possession. This has become increasingly important with the recent disturbing trend of identity theft occurring in the marketplace. Once someone gets hold of a person's Social Insurance Number, driver's licence, or bank account number, it is not that difficult for them to use that information to apply for other credit cards in that person's name and run up significant charges before the fraud is uncovered. I have seen cases where within 24 hours, loan applications, car purchases, and bank withdrawals have been completed against unsuspecting parties who have had their personal information compromised.

In the case of da Costa, decided December 19, 2001, the agent was found to have been careless in permitting sensitive personal information about a client to remain lying around on a cluttered desk, accessible to others, such that a third party was able to use that confidential information to fraudulently obtain a mortgage loan. This was found to be a violation of Rule 8 regarding confidential information. It was also found to be an example of unprofessional conduct under Rule 46. The agent had to pay a penalty of $5,000, with costs of $1,000.

In the case of Burt, decided September 15, 2003, Mr. Burt, the listing agent, disclosed to a potential buyer that the seller may have overpaid for the property initially and that was the reason they were firm on the asking price. The agent thought that the buyers might submit an offer through him and was surprised when the buyers used another agent to actually submit the offer. The penalty was $2,500, with costs of $1,000.

Weisleder's Wisdom on . . . CONFIDENTIALITY

1. Keep everything you hear from a client confidential.
2. Make sure that your clients are aware that this is in fact your policy regarding anything confidential.
3. Do not leave any confidential information unsecured where it can be accessed by third parties.

Primary Duty to Client (Rule 2)

A Member shall endeavor to protect and promote the best interests of the Member's Client. This primary obligation does not relieve the Member of the responsibility of dealing fairly, honestly, and with integrity with others involved in each Transaction.

Guiding Principles
Fiduciary Duty to Client:
2.1 A Member has a fiduciary duty, professionally and at law, to endeavor to protect and promote the interests of the Member's Client to the extent that he or she may ethically or legally do so. This relationship of trust means that the Member never puts the Member's interests above those of the Client. Competence, diligence, full disclosure, loyalty, confidentiality, and complete accounting are included in this duty.
2.2 Except in cases of Consensual Dual Agency, a Member does not act as a mediator between the Member's Client and the other Person involved in the Transaction. Rather, the Member advocates the Member's Client's position according to the Client's instructions.
2.3 A Member should inform a Client about the availability of a listed Property which is in the interests of the Client regardless of the fee or commission arrangement.

Honest Disclosure to Client:

2.4 A Member, in attempting to obtain a listing, should not knowingly misrepresent to the Seller the potential market value of a property. When attempting to enter into a Buyer Agency Agreement, a Member should not knowingly misrepresent to the Buyer the potential purchase price of a Property.

2.5 A Member should fully disclose to the Member's Client, at the earliest practical opportunity, any information that the Member knows or ought to know which could affect the decision to proceed with the transaction. The Member should disclose to the Member's Client the material steps that the Member takes on the Client's behalf.

2.6 A Member's primary duty is to the Member's Client. However, the Member also has a duty to deal fairly with the public, other Members, third parties, and the profession as a whole as represented by the Council. The Code of Ethics attempts to indicate how the Member can fulfill both sets of duties.

Fair Dealing with Customers:

2.7 A Member, when dealing with a Customer, should not mislead the Customer on matters pertaining to the Property or Transaction.

2.8 A Member, when dealing with a Customer, should exercise reasonable care when answering inquiries or giving information so that the answers or information are complete and accurate.

Fair Dealing with Third Parties:

2.9 A Member should provide competent, thorough, and skilled assistance when conferring with lawyers, mortgage lenders, home inspectors, surveyors, and other third parties that may be involved in the Transaction, and should cooperate with those persons, to facilitate the successful completion of any Transaction, to the extent practical without breaching any of the Member's duties to the Member's Client.

2.10 No Member should make a practice of Steering any Clients or Customers to a particular person for other services that may be required in connection with any Transaction.
2.11 All of the other Guiding Principles expand upon aspects of this primary duty.

If someone asked me how to be sure that I was always complying with this rule, I would answer as follows: "Disclose everything every time."

In the discipline decision of Galiegue, dated November 27, 2003, the agent was also the actual seller of a property and also acted on behalf of the buyer. The agent completed an SPIS form in which he indicated that he was not aware of any problems with the quality or quantity of water supplied to the property. He even signed a representation to this effect in the agreement itself. It turned out that the well in question was not even hooked up to the property until just prior to closing and that the water was not fit for human consumption. As proof that the water quality was acceptable, the agent tried to deliver a water sample taken over a year earlier that was not even from the same well.

There was clear evidence available to the panel that the agent did know there was a problem with the water and did not disclose it. The agent was found to have violated Rule 1, Ethical Behaviour; Rule 2, Primary Duty to Client; Rule 6, Written Transaction Agreements; Rule 10, Misrepresentation; Rule 11, Discovery of Facts; Rule 21, False Advertising; and Rule 46, Unprofessional Conduct. The fine against the agent and the broker, which was found liable under Rule 43, Broker Responsibility, was $20,000 each and $1,000 each in costs. Neither the broker nor the agent paid the penalty, so their memberships and registrations in the board were immediately terminated.

The buyer also commenced litigation proceedings against

the broker as a result of the same facts, which will involve many more years of stress for the agent regarding this action over and above what was associated with the discipline proceeding. All of this could have been avoided had he been open and honest, the cornerstone of this rule, in completing the SPIS statement.

As I have stated in Chapter 1, filling out an SPIS form will not get you into any trouble unless you deliberately complete it falsely. So long as you disclose everything that is material, you will not get into trouble if you do deliver the statement.

In the discipline decision of Yeung, decided July 19, 2001, the listing agent did not submit an offer from a buyer agent when he stood to benefit personally from a second offer where he could double end the commission. Besides being violations of Rule 1, Ethical Behaviour; Rule 46, Unprofessional Conduct; and Rule 14, Failure to Present All Offers, it was also deemed to be a violation of the primary duty of the agent to his own client. The penalty was $9,000, with $1,500 in costs.

In the case of Whittal, decided October 17, 2002, the listing agent did not present to his seller an offer for $75,000 that was received, and instead stated to the buyer agent that the seller would not look at an offer unless it was at least $120,000. No other offers were received and the seller ended up selling the property for $57,000. Besides violating Rule 14 in not presenting all offers to the client, the agent was deemed to have violated his primary duty to protect the client's interest. The penalty was $4,000, with costs in the amount of $1,750.

The agent in Kow's case, decided September 15, 2003, signed a listing agreement with the seller, and was also the agent for the buyer in an offer that was presented. The agent knew that there was a tenant on the property who had right of first refusal to buy the property and that she would not be paid commission if the tenant exercised this right. The buyer that was Ms. Kow's client approached the tenant on his own to purchase the property together with the tenant. The buyer agreed to pay Ms. Kow the commission that she would lose if the seller accepted the tenant's offer. Ms. Kow did not bring this information to the attention of the seller. The transaction with the tenant was completed, and Ms. Kow received commission from the buyer.

It was found by the panel that in not disclosing the foregoing information, she had violated Rule 2, Primary Duty to Client, to promote the best interests of the member's client. The penalty was $3,000, with costs of $1,000.

In the case of Richard B. Agent, decided June 12, 2001, the agent was careless in not following up on the deposit cheque from the buyer. The panel found that not taking active measures to obtain the deposit cheque from the buyers in a timely manner was a violation of Rule 2, in not properly protecting the interests of his client.

Weisleder's Wisdom on . . . PRIMARY DUTY TO CLIENT

1. Always treat the client as though they are your best friend: disclose everything.
2. Present all pertinent information, including all offers and counter-offers, to your clients.
3. Ensure that all obligations, conditions, and waivers provided for in any offer are followed through in a timely manner.

Disclosure of Role (Rule 3)

At the earliest practical opportunity, but no later than when the Member Accepts an Agency, a Member shall fully disclose in writing the role and nature of the service that the Member shall be providing to the Person. The Member shall also disclose the Member's role to others involved in the Transaction when appropriate.

Guiding Principles
Disclosure of Role:
3.1 A Member is strongly advised to obtain a written acknowl-edgement of the disclosure of the Member's role from the Person. Requesting a written acknowledgement brings home to the Person the seriousness of the disclosure. The written acknowledgement also provides evidence that the necessary disclosure has been made.
3.2 Disclosure of a Member's role includes identifying whether he or she is representing the Seller, the Buyer, or some other party to the Transaction. The Persons involved in the Transaction, including their representatives, should be clearly informed of the role of the Member in the Transaction.

Disclosure of Nature of the Service:
3.3 Disclosure of the "nature of service" includes explaining that the Member's primary responsibility is to protect and promote the interests of the Member's Client, but that this primary obliga-tion does not relieve the Member of the responsibility to deal fairly with all Parties to the Transaction.

Timing and Method of Disclosure:
3.4 The disclosure in this Rule should be made at the earliest practical opportunity in the relationship, but not later than when the Member Accepts an Agency, even if the written acknowl-edgement is obtained later in the relationship. A Person may disclose information to a Member that he or she might otherwise have kept confidential if the Person knew the Member's role, or, conversely, a Person may withhold information from the Member that he or she would otherwise have told the Member if the Person knew the Member's role.
3.5 The disclosure of role in this Rule should be included in writing in any Offer between the parties where the Member is representing a Party.

The main purpose of the rule sounds simple enough: That agents will explain to their clients as soon as possible the nature of the role and the services that they will be supplying in the transaction. When agents get into trouble with this rule, it is almost always in the very murky area of dual agency.

Dual agency is very confusing to clients. It can be very lucrative to agents. If you alone are acting as a dual agent, you will be double-ending the deal — receiving the commission payable to both the selling and buying agent. Duel agency can also arise if two agents from the same realty company represent the buyer and the seller. But how does one fairly represent both the buyer and the seller? The process begins by reviewing the dual agency provisions of the listing and buyer agency agreements as soon as possible with your seller and buyer.

We are told to disclose everything material in a transaction to our clients. In the context of dual agency, we are disclosing the material terms that we will *not* be disclosing to our clients. For example, when you act only for the seller and the buyer agent confides in you how high they think their client might go, you are obligated to tell this information to your seller, while at the same time telling the seller that you cannot guarantee the information, it is only what you have heard. However, in a dual agency situation, you cannot give this same information to the seller. It is very important that these provisions be reviewed carefully with both your buyer and seller clients so that they understand the consequences.

Many sellers believe it's a good thing when you act as a dual agent. They think it will be easier to ask you to reduce your commission, since you are double-ending. They fail to understand that there is also the restricted disclosure that will also take place. With respect to reducing your commission, I encourage you to think twice before agreeing to do this. You should not be punished for the fact that you have the connections or client base to be able to bring a buyer and seller together. Unless this was agreed to at the time the listing agreement was negotiated, you should refrain from cutting your commission, even if it means losing a transaction. Remember your own reputation or brand image. As discussed earlier, once you cut your commission one time, the word will get out and you will be pressured to always cut it.

Although there are certain restrictions on disclosure, this does not reduce an agent's obligations to both buyers and sellers for each of the other rules of the Code of Ethics. In fact, you can argue that there is an even greater obligation to protect both of your clients' interests in this situation, even if it means referring either or both of them to their respective lawyers for advice before they sign the agreement. For example, you should ensure that the Seller Property Information Statement has been accurately completed, delivered, and reviewed with the buyer before any agreement is signed.

In the discipline decision of Lowes, decided July 29, 2003, the agent acted as a dual agent without explaining his role in the transaction or obtaining the acknowledgement from the buyer as to his role. He failed to have the seller sign the SPIS form and also did not disclose to the buyers the fact that the driveway on the property belonged to the Ministry of Transportation. He also failed to suggest that the buyer obtain independent advice in reviewing the survey for the property in the event that he was not capable of doing so himself. The agent paid a penalty of $3,000 with costs of $1,350 for violating Rule 3.

There is always a potential for conflicts of interest when you represent both a buyer and a seller. In the case of Scocchia, decided January 9, 2003, the agent acted for the buyer and the seller on the sale of a property for the sum of $120,000. However, before the offer was even signed, the agent was also acting for the buyer on a potential resale of the same property to a third party for almost three times the value, without disclosing any of this information to the seller. Both transactions eventually closed on the same day, within minutes of each other, which was the point when the seller found out about the resale for the first time.

The discipline panel found it was clear that the agent was representing both the seller and the buyer. But it was incumbent on the agent to explain to both parties the nature of the services that he would be providing to each, including whether there would be any resale activity. He had even put the buyer at risk by permitting the buyer to sign the resale offer before he had actually completed the signing of the initial agreement with the seller. As soon as the agent heard of the third-party higher offer, he was in an immediate conflict of interest. He then proceeded to favour the interest of the buyer over the interest of the seller. The panel therefore found the agent to be in violation of Rules 1, 2, 3, 4, 10, and 11. The penalty was $20,000, with costs of $2,000, and the agent was put on immediate suspension for four months and on probation for two years.

In many cases, it is possible the agent does not think that they are representing the buyers, while the buyers mistakenly believe that the agent is acting for them. It's precisely for this reason that it is so important for agents to outline their roles and the services that they will provide as soon as possible upon meeting a client.

In the case of de Giacomo, decided December 16, 2002, the agent's name was posted on the sign at a sales office for new lots in a project. The buyers called the agent and expressed an interest in the property. Although the agent did not sign anything with the buyers, it was found by the panel that he was in fact representing the buyers in the transaction as well as the seller. He further permitted the buyers to write the deposit cheque payable directly to the seller when he knew that the seller was having financial difficulties with the project. The seller eventually went bankrupt and the buyers' deposit was lost. The penalty imposed was $15,000, with costs in the amount of $1,750.

The case of Dodge, dated March 31, 2004, was another situation involving an agent working for a builder. A buyer showed interest in a property, and the agent then prepared the offer and reviewed some of the provisions with the buyer, without explaining her role in the transaction. The buyer was told to review the offer with her lawyer, and a condition was inserted that the offer was conditional on the approval of the buyer's lawyer as well as on financing.

Although neither condition was satisfied, the agent was not cooperative in enabling the buyer to be released from the transaction. The committee found that there was an obligation on the part of the agent, even in this situation when the agent was obviously working for a builder, to confirm the role with the customer as soon as possible in writing and to properly explain who she was acting for in the transaction. The fine imposed on her was $4,000. This is a lesson to all agents who may act for builders. Make certain that all potential buyers are given written advice confirming that you will not be acting on their behalf, other than perhaps to complete the agreement itself, and that they are to obtain independent legal advice with respect to any matter contained in the offer.

In the case of McGinty, decided August 13, 2002, the agent acted as a dual agent without disclosing his role to the buyers. He further erred in describing the property as being 50 feet by 400 feet when it was only 50 feet by 308 feet. The panel noted that based on the evidence, the agent failed to properly explain his role in the transaction and took no measures to ensure that all documentation was provided to the buyers, and that he displayed little attention to details in completion and execution of documentation and failed to verify key facts relating to the property. The penalty imposed was $7,000, with costs of $2,450.

Weisleder's Wisdom on . . . DISCLOSURE OF ROLE

1. Explain all services that you will provide to a client as soon as possible, including any dual-agency possibilities.

2. When you are acting as a dual agent, be aware that there is almost a greater responsibility for you to take more care in carrying out all of your duties and obligations under the Code of Ethics.

3. Consider advising either or both of your clients to seek independent legal advice before signing the offer, especially when you act for a builder of new homes.

4. Complete the SPIS statement with your seller and review it with your buyers.

5. If any conflict of interest arises during the course of the transaction, immediately review the matter with your own broker and legal advisers to determine the most appropriate method to protect the interests of both of your clients.

Presentation of Offers and Multiple Offers (Rule 14)

A Member shall present all written Offers, including counter-offers, as objectively and as quickly as possible. The Member shall establish a system to ensure that all Offers are received and presented on a timely basis, including in the absence of the Member.

Guiding Principles

14.1 A Member should present all Offers promptly and objectively regardless of their source, content, or commission arrangement. Offers made through other Members or organizations should not be treated differently than Offers made through the Member or the Member's organization.

14.2 A Member should not withhold or delay the presentation of an Offer for the purpose of obtaining another Offer without the express written consent of the Client.

14.3 A Member should advise the Client about the facts and considerations that are relevant to the Client's decision to make or accept an Offer. However, a Member should leave the decision about the making or acceptance of an Offer to the Client alone.
14.4 Where there are competing Offers, the Member representing the Seller should inform the Persons making an Offer of the existence of all other Offers without disclosing their content unless directed to do so by the Seller in writing.
14.5 Sections 32 and 36 of the Real Estate and Business Brokers Act also apply here.

Section 32 − Breaking of contract prohibited
32. (1) No broker or salesperson shall induce any party to a contract for sale or rental of real estate to break the contract for the purpose of entering into another such contract.

Commission:
(2) Unless agreed to in writing by the seller, no broker is entitled to claim commission from the seller in respect of a trade in real estate if the real estate is to the knowledge of the broker covered by an unexpired listing agreement with another broker.

Date of Signing Listing or Offer:
(3) Every person signing a listing agreement or an agreement for sale or rental of real estate shall state with the person's signature the date upon which the signature was actually affixed.

Section 36 − Agreements to sell, purchase, etc.
36. Where a broker or salesperson has secured an acceptance of an offer to sell, purchase, exchange, lease, or rent real estate, the broker or salesperson shall require each of the parties to sign a sufficient number of copies of the agreement and the broker or salesperson shall retain one signed copy and shall forthwith deliver one signed copy to each of the parties.

Rule 14 brings up the recent phenomenon of bidding wars that break out when a property is listed in an extremely hot market. It is very important that agents prepare both the seller and their buyer clients in advance for this experience. Bidding wars are unusual and extremely stressful, and thus require the agent to be extra careful that they are taking all normal precautions with their clients, even under these trying conditions.

Before anyone submits an offer, the agent should review all the standard printed provisions with the customer, so that the only clauses that will have to be dealt with later are the conditions and the final sale or purchase price. The client will have to be educated that the seller does not necessarily have to deal with the highest offer, and in some cases may try to deal with more than one offer at the same time by making one a back-up offer, which would only take effect if another offer falls through.

The rules assume that agents will be honest with one another. It is required that an agent disclose the existence of multiple offers to all agents involved. This way their buyer customers can make the informed decision as to whether or not they wish to participate in this kind of free-for-all scenario. There is a duty for the listing agent to present all offers to the seller, and not attempt to only present offers where they may be double-ending the commission. The seller can ask that all offers be faxed instead of being presented in person, which can cause additional problems, especially when the listing broker is also presenting one of the offers themselves. It is important that all this information be disclosed in advance to your client, so that they can make an informed decision as to whether or not to participate in this bidding process.

Let's assume the offer is to be presented in person and you are told in advance that there will be multiple offers. What do you do if you arrive on the listing and there are no other offers present? It is possible that the seller's agent did not mislead you but that the buyers with the other offers changed their minds. In this circumstance, prior to your presenting the offer, you have a duty to advise your buyer client as to this new development and to then take instructions as to whether or not the offer is to be presented.

In many multiple-offer situations, there will be pressure on buyers to submit a clean offer, with no conditions, because these will obviously be favoured by the seller. If you are considering doing this, you must be very careful to obtain written instructions from your buyer. You must also ensure that they are adequately protected, if possible. For example, by pre-qualifying the buyer for financing, it may be possible to shorten or eliminate the time period for the financing condition, such that the only condition would be for the financial institution to approve or qualify the property itself. It is still advisable to always conduct a home inspection. In this situation, advise the buyer to obtain a home inspection before they submit the offer, so that they can be satisfied with the condition of the property instead of taking it in an "as is" condition. The seller should be accommodating to this kind of request. If the buyer refuses your advice about obtaining the home inspection, document these instructions in writing, because the buyer is unlikely to remember this conversation the moment they discover defects in the property after closing.

From an emotional standpoint, a multiple-offer listing is almost like an auction process. In most cases, agents will deliberately list a property under market value in order to generate multiple offers. We have seen properties listed at $399,000 in Toronto that are sold subsequently for $475,000 a few days after the listing began. This can cause a tremendous emotional strain on buyers as well as sellers when the stakes become so high and multiple parties are involved. That is why it is so important that buyers are educated in advance as to what to expect in these kinds of situations, so that they will not be disappointed later if their offer is not accepted.

In the discipline decision of Ash, dated June 6, 2002, the buyer broker phoned Mr. Ash to inquire whether there were competing offers and was told that there were none. Mr. Ash did however insist that the offer remain open until October 5, 2001. On that day, at 7:30 p.m., the buyer agent was told that the seller had in fact accepted another offer — an offer from another client of Mr. Ash.

Although not technically a violation of Rule 14, since all offers were in fact presented to the seller, this action was deemed a violation of Rule 1 (1), Ethical Behaviour; Rule 2, Primary Duty to Client; and Rule 46, Unprofessional Conduct. The penalty was $3,500 with costs of $1,500 against the agent.

> ### Weisleder's Wisdom on . . .
> ### PRESENTATION OF OFFERS AND MULTIPLE OFFERS
>
> 1. Always present all offers as soon as they are received, regardless of whether they are from your own office or another broker's office.
> 2. Disclose the existence of multiple offers to all agents that are involved.
> 3. Prepare your clients for potential bidding wars, including the stress that is likely to occur. This will help keep them calm in what can be an intense process.
> 4. Protect your buyer clients by satisfying any conditions in advance, where possible.
> 5. Document instructions if you are told to waive or delete conditions that have not yet been satisfied.

This chapter's review of the RECO rules, and examples in which they were not followed, should help you make your practices as an agent more professional and help you bulletproof yourself against disciplinary as well as potential legal proceedings. At the same time, by following these principles, you will end up with long-term, satisfied loyal customers. Now let's turn to new legislation that you should be aware of, on privacy.

Casting Light on the New Privacy Act

As of January 1, 2004, the new federal Privacy Act became applicable to most commercial activities in Canada. The Act has created much concern in many industries, including real estate, regarding the consequences of not complying with the new privacy rules.

Real estate is a good example of an industry that uses personal information on a daily basis. Therefore, all real estate agents and brokers should understand their rights and obligations under the Privacy Act. There are two main reasons for you to do so:

 • To ensure that you do not violate any of the Act's provisions and invite an audit by the Privacy Commissioner's office in Ottawa (which I assure you is not kept private!)

 • To learn how to use these Privacy principles as a marketing advantage in your practice

Before looking at the implications of the Act for you as a real estate agent or broker, let's consider the Act itself and what gave rise to it.

A BIRD'S-EYE VIEW OF THE ACT

The legislation passed by the Federal Government is called the Personal Information Protection and Electronic Documents Act and is commonly referred to as "PIPEDA." The Act is divided into two parts. The first part deals with the protection of personal information. The second part promotes electronic commerce by providing for the use of electronic means to communicate or record information or transactions. Real estate professionals should focus on the former.

The main purpose of the first part of the Act is stated in section 3:

> The purpose of this part is to establish, in an era in which technology increasingly facilitates the circulation and exchange of information, rules to govern the collection, use, and disclosure of personal information in a manner that recognizes the right of privacy of individuals with respect to their personal information and the need of organizations to collect, use, or disclose personal information for purposes that a reasonable person would consider appropriate in the circumstances.

The creation of the Internet was the driving force behind worldwide privacy legislation. Countries were not only concerned about how businesses shared consumer information with other businesses in the same country, but also about the implications when potential businesses had the ability to transmit this information to other companies all over the world.

The first action taken in this regard was by the European Union. Countries in Europe would not do business with each other unless the other particular countries passed specific laws related to privacy, similar to the principles of PIPEDA. When Canada sought to join this electronic commerce union, they were required to pass a similar privacy law, and this is why

PIPEDA was passed in its current form. The law came into effect on January 1, 2001, but was only applicable to federally regulated businesses such as the telecom industry and the banking industry. The rest of the country's businesses became regulated effective January 1, 2004.

Under the Canadian Constitution, matters of personal information are typically under the jurisdiction of the provincial governments. In Ontario, for example, the government has passed the Consumer Reporting Act, which deals with how consumer reporting agencies, commonly known as credit bureaus, handle the personal and credit information of customers. Accordingly, there is an express provision in PIPEDA that it will no longer be effective in a province once that province passes its own privacy legislation. Quebec, Alberta, and British Columbia have already passed privacy legislation, and Ontario was expected to pass its own privacy law at the end of 2004. The Ontario Government is now taking the position that it will wait a little longer to see how the federal legislation is interpreted in practice before introducing their own privacy legislation. In any event, the principles of all the privacy laws passed to date are alike.

Personal information is any information that can identify an individual, excluding their name, business address, and business phone number. In the real estate business, any facts about a person's home, including the property address and its sale price, are considered personal information because that information can be used to identify the owner of the property. It makes no difference that you can look up this information in other public databases, such as the local land registry office. You can only use personal information with the consent of the individual.

WHAT GAVE RISE TO THE ACT

Why was the Act introduced in the first place? One of the main objectives of privacy legislation is to protect ordinary consumers from invasions of their privacy, including the sharing of personal information about them without their permission. Advances in electronic technology have made this an all-pervasive problem in many countries.

If I asked you to indicate what you felt was the most annoying invasion of your privacy on a daily basis, you would probably answer telemarketing calls at home, closely followed by spam e-mails, unwanted fax advertisements, and the direct mail and junk mail that cascades out of your mail box. How did these people and businesses obtain your telephone and fax numbers, your e-mail and home addresses? Initially, most telemarketers simply went through the phone book to obtain this information. However, after they were successful in selling their products or services to a list of customers, this list became very valuable information, which the telemarketers then sold to others. The Privacy Act prevents this type of selling of lists going forward, unless individuals have consented to this in advance.

I also receive many annoying recorded voice messages telling me to call a number to hear about a great product or marketing opportunity. I used to wonder why any telemarketer would think that anyone would ever bother to call this number, as I usually hang up the phone within two seconds of realizing I'm on the other end of a canned pitch. I later learned that telemarketers are more interested in when we pick up the phone than in how we respond to the pitch. When we pick up the phone is valuable information that they can share with other telemarketers. (I have also learned that you can abort this fact-gathering by pressing the # key six times before hanging up.)

Canada does not have a national "do not call" list. However, you can go to the Web site of the Canadian Marketing

Association (CMA), www.the-cma.org, and register your phone and fax numbers and mailing address if you do not wish to receive any further invasions of your privacy. The list is updated every three months and then circulated to all of the members of the CMA. About 80% of all telemarketers in Canada are members of the CMA and follow this list. The penalty for not following the list is having your number disconnected by the local phone service provider. So while I cannot guarantee that you will not receive a fax from Nigeria telling you that you can have $75 million transferred into your trust account by paying a small $5,000 "transfer" fee, you will be able to cut down on most of these unwanted communications.

The U.S. experience with their own "do not call" list demonstrates just how annoyed the U.S. consumer is with these kinds of invasions. When the "do not call" list was introduced, it was expected that two million consumers would sign up. As of March 31, 2004, over 58 million consumers in that country had signed up, and it is expected that eventually 100 million will add their names to the list. As a direct result of these lists, and the penalties associated with calling someone who is registered on the list, several U.S. call centres have closed, and companies are reducing their workforce in these areas.

Recent surveys have shown that 70% of Canadians would consider adding their names if a similar list was established in Canada. The Canadian Marketing Association expects the federal government to introduce Do Not Call Legislation either in 2005 or 2006. As realtors engage in many forms of marketing their services, they will have to be very mindful of these realities in the marketplace.

THE PRIVACY ACT AND THE
REAL ESTATE INDUSTRY

In the real estate industry, the question that you have to ask yourself is: "Are my actions going to bother someone or invade their privacy to such an extent that they will bring a complaint to the Privacy Commissioner in Ottawa or launch a court action for damages?" You can see on the Privacy Commissioner's Web site (www.privcom.gc.ca) that there have already been many investigations and decisions by the Privacy Commissioner's office as a result of complaints made by consumers claiming their privacy has been invaded.

The Real Estate Council of Ontario (RECO) publishes a similar list of decisions at its own Web site (www.reco.on.ca), regarding any discipline proceedings that have been brought against agents. As I have stated in previous chapters, one of the main reasons to follow the principles in this book is to avoid a claim being made against you that could lead to your being included on this Privacy Wheel of Misfortune. Obviously, you want to avoid the negative publicity, fines, and penalties that arise when you become the subject of a disciplinary proceeding under RECO or another provincial real estate council. You also do not want to take a star turn on the Privacy Commissioner's Web site.

Any consumer is free to complain to the Privacy Commissioner's office about your actions. Once the Commissioner decides to investigate or conduct a privacy audit, it will cause you the same anxiety, stress, and expense as an income tax audit. The fines and penalties can be as high as $100,000 for companies, $20,000 for individuals. Since this legislation is still in the early stages, the Privacy Commissioner's office is trying to mediate situations between complaining consumers and the allegedly offending organizations, and, more importantly, to ensure that the organizations in question have adequate privacy policies in place going forward so that similar complaints do not arise in the future.

Many agents say to me: "You make a big point that we should disclose everything that is material and relevant to my principal, then you turn around and tell me that I can't disclose certain things because they are 'personal and confidential.' How can we reconcile these two principles?" In fact, privacy law is just an extension of common sense principles that we already use on a daily basis in the business. Many agents act as dual agents on a regular basis, representing both buyers and sellers. When you act as a dual agent, you are not permitted to tell a seller client how high the buyer may go, even if the buyer confides this information to you. Most sellers will tell you that this is the most material information they could think of, yet you do not have to disclose it. The reason? When you mention the dual agency relationship to your clients in the first place, you explain very clearly that you will *not* be disclosing these facts. In other words, you are disclosing what you will not disclose. In this way, you are in fact fulfilling the obligations regarding full and complete disclosure. Privacy law is a further extension of these same principles, in that you are telling someone in advance what you will be using their information for.

Virtually 95% of all real estate buyers require a mortgage to complete their purchase. The first thing the bank will request is a credit check on the prospective buyer. For the bank to do a credit check, it must get a written consent from the buyer because the bank will be basing its decision on the customer's personal information. The main source of information for the bank is the customer's credit history.

Most people across Canada who have ever applied for a credit card or loan have their own unique credit history at the credit bureaus. How the credit bureaus use this information is governed by the Consumer Reporting Act in Ontario and similar legislation introduced by the other provinces. For example, this legislation says that when you ask a customer for permission to do a credit check, the font of the sentence must be **bolded** and of a certain height so as to come to the attention of the customer. (That is why the printed provision number 23, "Consumer Reports," in the agreement of purchase and sale in Ontario is bolded while the other printed provisions are not.) The legislation and this provision give sellers the opportunity to have a credit check done on buyers if they are worried whether the buyers have the ability to complete the proposed transaction.

Under the same credit protection legislation, consumers are able to access their own files, by making an appointment with one of the credit reporting agencies. These agencies usually require photo identification before releasing this information, because it is very private and sensitive. An individual also has the right to have the information in their file changed if it is incorrect, by submitting support material from the relevant bank, landlord, or business.

10 PRINCIPLES OF PRIVACY

The Privacy Act codifies 10 principles of privacy that were first introduced by the Canadian Standards Association in 1996. If you and your organization understand the applicability of these 10 principles, you should be able to deal successfully with any related privacy issue that you will face in the course of your business.

But first, consider these three overriding principles to understanding the 10 principles of privacy. If these three are understood, the rest will merely serve as further clarification. The three principles are:

• Appoint someone in your office to be responsible for all privacy issues, including handling any complaints from the public, educating all staff, and protecting any personal information in your or your office's possession.

• Disclose to your customer, either before or at the time you obtain their personal information, what you will be using their personal information for.

• Obtain the consent of the customer.

And now . . . the 10 principles of privacy, including examples of how these relate to the real estate industry.

Principle 1 — Accountability

An organization is responsible for personal information under its control and shall designate an individual or individuals who are accountable for the organization's compliance [with the principles of the Act].

Every real estate office must have its own Privacy Officer, someone responsible for all issues related to privacy in that office. If that office's number comes up for an audit, the Privacy Commissioner's office will want to know who this officer is. There is no requirement that the Privacy Officer be a real estate broker. It can be an agent in the office or even an administrative worker. The key is whether this person has the authority to deal with any privacy issues that come up and is ensuring that everyone in the office is following the privacy policies set up by your office. (Many businesses give someone a new title when they do not want to give them a raise. This could guide you in giving someone the new title of Privacy Officer!)

Principle 2 — Identifying Purposes

The purposes for which personal information is collected shall be identified by the organization at or before the time the information is collected.

This is the main principle of all privacy legislation. You must tell someone what you plan to use their personal information for either before or at the time you collect the information. In a typical listing situation, you are collecting personal information about a seller — facts about the property being sold and the listing price to be offered. You must identify this to the seller at the time you obtain the listing, either verbally or in writing.

Accordingly, the listing agreements nationwide have been modified such that the seller is now providing consent to the agent to use and disclose all the personal information about the seller's property in order to sell his or her property. This consent gives the agent the right to let everyone know that the property is for sale, by any means necessary.

While this may seem obvious in a listing situation, it becomes less clear in other instances. An example would be the sign-in sheet that buyers are asked to sign when they visit an open house. The buyer is usually told that the reason for the request for the buyer's name and address is for "security reasons." The seller needs to know who was visiting the property. What usually happens a few days later is that the listing agent decides to contact the potential buyers by telephone to see if they are still interested in that property. He may also be looking to solicit these customers to purchase other properties that he may have listed. In either case, he did not identify the purpose for this call when the customer originally signed in at the open house. He has not been given permission to make this call, and is in fact now bothering the customer at home. Is he much different from the rest of the annoying telemarketers?

This situation can be easily avoided by stating on the sign-in sheet that the buyer also consents to being contacted by the agent after the visit to discuss the property or other properties. The agent has identified the purpose of the request for personal information and no complaint can be made. No one will object to your calling them at home if they have given you permission in advance to do just that.

Can an agent market to a seller whose listing has expired? This personal information is available on most MLS services. However, when the seller consented to list the property, she only gave permission to the agent to do anything necessary to sell the property "during the listing." She did not give permission for other agents to use this personal information to solicit her after the listing expired. Accordingly, as this purpose was not identified or agreed to at the time of the listing, contacting this seller is a violation of privacy law.

Many agents have asked whether it is okay to call the seller and ask for permission to send them information. What you must remember is that just telephoning the seller as a result of your use of the personal information is already a violation.

The conundrum of how to contact the seller reminds me of something that happened at a major brokerage house. The president of the company called the bond trader desk inquiring what the interest rate spread was that day. The trader replied in irritation, "Don't you realize how busy I am?" The president replied, "Have you any idea who you are talking to? I am the president of the bank." The trader gulped and said, "Do you have any idea who you are talking to?" The president replied, "No." "Good," the trader said and hung up.

You will have to make your own determination or risk assessment as to whether or not someone will complain as a result of this kind of action. Most sellers have a reasonable expectation that they will be contacted after their listing expires and thus are not too upset when it happens. However, some may in fact be very bothered and could complain.

In Saskatchewan, the listing agreement has been amended such that the seller does in fact agree that they may be contacted after the listing expires. While that does seem to solve the problem, there are concerns whether this type of consent is appropriate in the context of the listing agreement as a whole and whether it is being properly explained to the seller at the time the listing is signed. However, the amendment is an attempt to deal with the issue of contacting a vendor after a listing expires, where there is no express consent to do so.

Many have asked whether agents are permitted, as a way of making contacts, to offer their services to owners who are trying to sell the property themselves, via the common "For Sale by Owner" (FSBO) signs. The answer is that you can contact these owners. Others question whether you can contact them if their sign states "No Agents." In my view, you can still contact them, by saying something like, "I understand that you have advertised that you have no agent. Well don't worry, I am here." On a more serious note, you should keep track of how long a FSBO is on the market. Once it is over four weeks, there is an opportunity to approach the owner by saying something such as, "I am trying to be updated on all market activity in this area. Would you be offended if I took a quick look at your home?" Most owners will not complain with this approach.

Another difficult issue concerns a real estate appraisal. Typically, an appraisal consists of sold prices and listing prices of comparable properties. In most jurisdictions in Canada, when someone now lists a property on a multiple listing service, they are giving permission for the listing information and subsequent sale of the property to be used in any future comparative market analysis (CMA) or appraisal. That purpose has been identified in the listing agreement. However, for any sale that happened prior to 2004, the owner did not give permission for the sale price to be included in this appraisal or CMA report, nor was the purpose identified at the time of the listing. For any such property, appraisers and real estate agents are now being advised to quote only a range of prices without identifying the actual address with a specific price. This reasoning is difficult for most agents and appraisers to accept due to the following:

- The information about sale price of virtually any property is available at the local land registry office.
- The seller probably relied on a similar appraisal report when they purchased the property in the first place.
- The context of an appraisal or CMA report is typically confidential between an agent and a private customer or between an appraiser and their own client. It is not intended to be released to the general public.
- This use of personal information is not likely to bother any person identified by the information.

In order to be extra cautious, you should obtain from your clients a written statement that they will keep the contents of the CMA report confidential. It could be as simple as the one-line statement: "I agree to keep the contents of this CMA report confidential and not to disclose the contents to any third party." An example of confidentiality provisions can be found in Appendix C.

In my view, the combination of these powerful arguments and obtaining a confidentiality agreement would be looked at favourably should the issue ever go to the Privacy Commissioner for adjudication. The risk of someone complaining in this situation is very low, and it will become even lower as we move forward and more and more sales that are the subject of the CMA occur after January 1, 2004. For this reason, most appraisers have not changed their form of appraisal at all, continuing to use the same methods. What it comes down to is that most sellers would not be bothered if the sale price of a home that they sold some time ago is included in someone else's appraisal report, which is being used to determine the value of similar homes in the area.

It is a very different situation, however, if a nosy neighbour calls your office the day after you have sold your seller's house and asks you what the house sold for. I believe that disclosing this information without the seller's permission could bother the seller. Being cavalier about this kind of personal information to virtual strangers makes you look unprofessional. You should instead consider using privacy in this situation as a positive marketing opportunity. Imagine saying the following to the nosy neighbour:

> As you know, the sale price of the home is personal information of our customer. We value this information and keep it private. If you are interested in listing your own home, we would be happy to share the same marketing expertise that we used to sell your neighbour's property to serve your own needs.

Instead of considering privacy as a barrier to your marketing and selling efforts, use it as a positive marketing opportunity wherever possible.

A favourite marketing tool of an agent after a successful sale of a property is to send out cards announcing that they have sold the property at, for example, 102% of the listing price. This value being advertised is in fact personal information. In a typical listing agreement, the agent's marketing purpose has not been identified to the seller, and therefore, it is not permissible under privacy law. What is permissible is to state that you have sold a home in the area or to say that you have sold three homes in the area with an average price of, for example, $300,000. If the purpose had been identified and agreed to by the seller, then you would be able to send out the cards immediately after the sold sign is placed on the property. (I will demonstrate under Principle 8 a method in which you are able to obtain this consent of the seller very easily, again by using privacy as a marketing opportunity.)

Marketing your sales is further complicated by another issue: whether you also require the permission of the buyer to advertise the successful sale of a property by a listing seller. The listing agent only has a relationship with a seller, not a buyer (except in dual agency circumstances). Yet the sale price of a property is also the personal information of a buyer. Dealing strictly with privacy law, you could make a strong argument that you only need the permission of the seller to do this kind of successful marketing. However, most organizations governing the real estate industry, such as the Real Estate Council of Ontario, take a different view as to what consents are required for proper advertising.

Looking at decisions issued by RECO, it appears that the sale price of a home is the personal information of the seller from the date the agreement is entered into until the date of closing or title transfer. After closing, this same personal information belongs to both the seller and the buyer. So here's the distinction. Once the sold sign goes in the ground, you require the permission only of the seller to send out listing cards. After closing, however, you require the permission of both the seller and the buyer.

In the RECO discipline decision regarding Siu, reported December 29, 2003, Mr. Siu faced proceedings for having violated several RECO rules relating to improper advertising. The main violations were that he advertised that he "sold a house every three days," his name was larger than his broker's in several advertisements, and he did not obtain the permission of buyers to advertise that he had sold their properties, after closing.

The safest practice, therefore, would be to obtain the permission of both your seller and your buyer before you do any marketing of the successful sale of your property.

Principle 3 — Obtaining Consent

The knowledge and consent of a customer are required for the collection, use, or disclosure of personal information except where inappropriate.

This third rule is the easy answer to all privacy questions. If you obtain the prior consent of the customer to whatever you are planning to do, you will not have any complaint later. The secret is to obtain this consent in a positive manner, using privacy not as a restriction on your business but as a marketing opportunity for your business.

We have seen that the most common form of consent in the real estate industry is now found in the listing agreement itself, whereby the customer gives the listing agent consent to use whatever means possible to effect the sale of the property, including the ability to disclose personal information about the property to anyone who can assist in selling the property. A copy of the relevant listing language is disclosed below, found in section 11 of the Ontario Real Estate Association Listing Agreement, and has been adopted by most real estate boards in Canada:

> The seller consents to the collection, use, and disclosure of personal information by the Broker for the purpose of listing and marketing the Property including, but not limited to, listing and advertising the Property using any medium including the Internet; disclosing Property information to perspective buyers, brokers, salespersons, and others who may assist in the sale of the Property; such other use of seller's personal information as is consistent with listing and marketing of the Property. The Seller consents, if this is an MLS listing, to placement of the listing information and sales information by the Broker into the database of the appropriate MLS system(s) and acknowledges that the MLS database is the property of the board(s) and can be licensed, resold, or

otherwise dealt with by the board(s). The Seller further acknowledges that the board(s) may: distribute the information to any
persons authorized to use such service which may include other
brokers, government departments, appraisers, municipal organizations, and others; market the Property, at its option, in any medium,
including electronic media; compile, retain, and publish any statistics including historical MLS data which may be used by licensed
board members to conduct comparative market analyses; and make
such other use of the information as the board deems appropriate
in connection with the listing, marketing, and selling of real estate.

The seller is thus agreeing to the agent's conveyance of personal information to any other agent or other person for the
purpose of selling the property. If the property is listed on
MLS, the seller authorizes the MLS service to disclose the information to any other party at its discretion, including other
board members, government agencies, appraisers, and others.
The seller further consents to subsequent sales data being
retained by the board and compiled and used by any other
member for a comparative market analysis, as discussed under
Principle 2.

The seller now understands the identified purpose of the
disclosure of personal information — to sell his property —
and he has given his consent by signing the listing agreement.

If you want to use information associated with the sign-in
sheet at an open house, you must obtain the customer's consent on the document itself. It should be informed consent:
consumers must understand what they are consenting to.
While there has been much debate as to how to obtain this
consent, two methods have been deemed acceptable by the
Privacy Commission: opt-in consent and opt-out consent.

• In opt-in consent, consumers must check off a box indicating
that they agree to have their personal information disclosed for a

particular purpose. In the open house sign-in sheet example, the clause would read as follows:

The undersigned consents to X using my personal information to contact me about this property and other similar properties.

The consumer would then check off a box beside the statement, agreeing to receive the information. This method is stronger proof that the person has consented.

• In an opt-out consent, unless the consumer checks off the box, he has agreed to accept the information. For example:

You agree that X may use your personal information to send you information about this property or similar properties. If you do not wish to receive this information, please check the attached box.

In this case, customers who have not checked the box are deemed to have consented to your sending the information.

What about the mailing lists that we have assembled over the years? Can we continue marketing to these clients, if we are not sure whether we have obtained their consent in the first place? There is also the concept of implied consent. If you can demonstrate that there is implied consent within the client relationship for you to send information, you can continue to do so. Therefore, if you have been using your mailing list in the past to send your customers cards, calendars, and marketing information, you can continue to do so, without any further consent. This is the concept of "grandfathering" that the legislation recognizes. However, if you intend to change the use of this information (sell or give it to a third party), the consent of each of your clients would be required. You are advised, as you market to customers in the present "privacy age," to include the following opt-out language in your marketing material:

We value your personal information. If you wish to be removed from our mailing list, or have any other questions about the use of personal information, please contact us at . . .

I am not suggesting that you insert this kind of language on your Christmas cards. However, you should include it whenever you do a targeted mailing or e-mail marketing campaign. It would be difficult for any recipient to make a complaint when you have given them the means to stop receiving this kind of information.

As discussed under Principle 2, if you would like to send out cards advertising the fact that you have had a successful sale of a client's property, the easiest way to do this is to obtain the customer's permission, using the opt-in or opt-out forms of consent. You should try to obtain this consent as soon as you get the listing agreement signed. It can be as simple as one sentence saying: "I agree that you may use my personal information to market the successful sale of my property." By getting this consent in advance, you avoid any possibility of bothering the client later when you do in fact advertise how successful you were in selling the property.

Principle 4 – Limiting Collection

Members shall limit the collection of personal information to that which is necessary for the purposes identified.

There is no reason to collect personal information beyond what is required to carry out your agency responsibilities. As we will see under Principle 7, there is a duty to protect and safeguard personal information that is in your possession. Therefore, because of the potential damage that could result from your improper or accidental disclosure of personal information, you should not obtain information that you don't absolutely require.

For example, there is no need to collect a customer's social insurance number unless you expect that the interest earned on a deposit will exceed $50, in which case you would have to issue a T5 slip to the customer. There is no other reason to keep this confidential information.

Principle 5 — Limiting Use, Disclosure, and Retention
Members shall use or disclose personal information only for the reason it was collected, except with the consent of the consumer or as required by law.

On the surface, this appears to be an easy concept to understand. Unless the information is required by law, you cannot disclose personal information unless you have received permission from your customer or client. We tend to associate "required by law" to mean if required pursuant to a legal warrant or subpoena or similar demand. But consider if the seller says the following sorts of things to you:

"This used to be a grow house operation, but I have cleaned it up so no one has to know about it. It's personal information."

"A sexual predator lives in the basement apartment next door, but that's okay, that's personal information. Besides, he hasn't bothered anyone for the last six months."

"The prior owner committed suicide in the house but that's a private family matter. It's no one else's business."

Under privacy, you could argue that if the seller is saying you do not have permission to disclose this information, you would probably have to follow his instructions. However, think about this for a minute. Is this *material* information that *you* would want to know if *you* were buying the property? If the answer is yes, then you know that you should be disclosing this information to a buyer. Remember the concept of full disclosure discussed in Chapter 1; no privacy rule can change a seller's obligation to disclose what should be disclosed.

There is much debate as to whether a stigma house should have that fact disclosed. If you disclose everything, you cannot be successfully sued by any buyer. You do not want to be a part of any lawsuit or discipline proceeding, so disclose everything, whether it is a suicide, accidental or natural death, group home in the neighbourhood, damage to the property itself, or anything related to it. If your seller is pressuring you not to disclose this information, your answer should be, "Please go and get yourself another agent." It is very likely that if something does go wrong, the seller will have disappeared and you will be left with a lawsuit on your hands. Do not be fooled by a seller's attempt to use privacy as a cover-up for something illegal. Take no part in this scheme and you will be rewarded with very few complaints in your career.

Principle 6 — Accuracy
Members shall keep personal information as accurate, complete, current, and relevant as necessary of its identified purpose.

When you are relying on information to make a decision about a consumer, you must keep that information as accurate and current as possible. For example, anytime you apply for a mortgage loan or credit card, you must pass a credit check. The laws and regulations surrounding the credit reporting agencies in Ontario, or credit bureaus as they are commonly called, are governed by the Provincial Consumer Reporting Act, but the principles relate very closely to the new privacy legislation. The credit reporting agencies are constantly updating their credit files with current information, because they understand that companies are relying upon this information in order to make decisions about whether to grant credit to a particular consumer.

If you are acting as a property manager for a landlord, you also have this obligation. You must keep your tenant files as current as possible with relevant information, because the landlord will be relying on this information when making decisions affecting the ongoing relationship with a tenant — relocation of the tenant into a different unit, sharing of any capital improvements, and decisions whether to grant any extension of the lease upon renewals.

Principle 7 — Protecting Information

Members shall protect personal information with safeguards appropriate to the sensitivity of the information.

It is common sense that if we are entrusted with the personal information of clients, we should be doing our best to protect this information from being released to third parties. This is especially true given the recent phenomenon of identity theft and the fraudulent duplication of social insurance numbers, credit cards, and automatic banking cards to defraud consumers and financial institutions. We have read about hackers getting through an organization's firewall computer protection for the purpose of obtaining sensitive financial information of the company's customers in order to orchestrate this type of identity theft. It has caused companies to spend enormous sums of money ensuring that their computer systems are protected from outside threats. As an extra precaution, only a few people within the organization understand the systems that protect the company information. Any company that gathers personal information from consumers needs to protect this information. The nature of the protection that your organization will need will depend on the sensitivity of the information you are collecting.

If you are careless in how you safeguard and protect personal information, you may be held liable in a civil action. There is always the possibility that a consumer can take you to civil court to assert a claim for damages in relation to violation of their privacy rights. While it is debatable whether most violations under the privacy principles will give rise to a civil claim for damages, the careless release of sensitive personal information could lead directly to losses and damages suffered by the consumer. It would form a logical basis for a claim for damages against you in a civil court.

How should your organization protect the personal information that you collect? As with your entire privacy policy, you must make all employees in the organization aware of the importance of maintaining the confidentiality and security of personal information. Sensitive personal information should be accessible *only* to those who need to know it.

Many of these principles of protection are just common sense. You should conduct an inventory of your respective offices to see where sensitive information is stored. If it is in a cabinet, then the cabinet should be locked and accessible only to those who need the information contained in those files. Fax machines should never be in an open environment. They should be under the care and control of a specific person who can then distribute the faxes to the persons for whom the information is applicable.

I heard about a Privacy Officer in one real estate office who took her responsibility so seriously that she locked the fax machine in the closet after she left the office at 5:00 p.m. That's a bit extreme. We all understand that a realtor needs access to their fax machines at all times, due to many deals that are signed and accepted at all hours of the night. Yet it would be a good idea to have another person appointed to be responsible for this information in the evening hours — it's that important.

The Privacy Commissioner's office rendered a decision recently that it is not sufficient that you throw sensitive personal information into the wastepaper basket. Personal information should in fact be shredded before being thrown out. This brings into question your company's relationship to the cleaning companies that enter your offices, often in the evenings when no one is there. It is quite possible that they may obtain access to sensitive personal information. Many companies are now requiring cleaning suppliers to sign confidentiality agreements. All realtors should practise the proper disposal of personal information.

Principle 8 — Openness Concerning Policies and Practices

Members shall make readily available to consumers specific information about their policies and practices relating to the management of personal information.

This principle states that each organization needs to have a privacy policy that clearly sets out what your company does with personal information. Furthermore, this policy should be available in the event anyone asks you about it.

A copy of a standard privacy policy is found in Appendix B. It details the essential information you need in order to comply with privacy obligations. It's very important for every employee in your office to read and understand your privacy policy and to be able to explain it to any consumer who asks about it.

In my view, you should be doing much more with your privacy policy. It can be a great marketing opportunity for your company. Put your privacy policy into a brochure and show it to your sellers as early in the listing process as possible. Use the brochure to show potential customers how much you value their personal information and how it will only be used for the purpose of selling the property. Have your clients then sign the brochure, confirming that they agree with your privacy policy terms, as shown in Appendix D.

You could go even further. In your policies, include language that makes it clear that you will also be using this personal information to market the successful sale of the property after the agreement is signed. You may go still further and say that you will post this information on your own company Web site as a service to all your customers. Sellers should not object if you explain this in the following way:

> Our firm values and respects the personal information of our customers. We use it only to do everything we can to sell your property and then to let others know how successful we were in selling your property.

It should then not be difficult to have your seller consent to your privacy policy terms. Just like that you have obtained the permission of your seller customer to send out listing cards announcing your successful sale of the property. You should consider this, too: Whenever buyer agents call to tell you that they will be bringing in an offer, fax them a copy of your privacy policy and ask them to have it signed by the buyer before the offer is submitted. If the buyer agent explains this properly, the buyers should not be caused much concern, especially since buyer agents should be explaining their own privacy policies to their own customers. In this way, you have now obtained the permission of buyers to market the successful sale of their property as well.

You may now have solved all the privacy issues relating to your ability to market the successful sale of a property. If all real estate offices make a coordinated effort to adopt this marketing practice, most agents will be able to market the subsequent successful sale of any property without any further permissions required and, more importantly, without violating any privacy principles.

A related issue is how long agents should retain files and personal information. The obvious answer is that you should shred or otherwise destroy the information as soon as you no longer need it. There is no set rule as to how long information should be retained. However, most financial aspects of transactions, such as sale prices and commissions earned, will need to be retained for income tax purposes for at least seven years, based on guidelines prescribed by the Income Tax Act of Canada and the recommendations of your own company accountants. Ask for guidance from your legal advisers and insurers as to how long you should retain information due to the possibility of legal actions being commenced against your firm based on a file that may have been closed years earlier.

With respect to computer information, my advice is that you print important e-mails and attachments and file this information instead of storing everything electronically and then having to worry about where the information is stored, whether it was properly backed up, or whether some new computer virus will destroy it in the future.

Principle 9 – Consumer Access

Upon request, members shall inform a customer of the existence, use, and disclosure of his or her personal information and shall give the individual access to that information.

This is another common-sense principle of privacy law: A consumer should be permitted access to whatever information of theirs that you have in your files. As we discussed in Principle 7, Protecting Information, this has long been the accepted practice with respect to your own credit information on file with the consumer reporting agencies or credit bureaus. All of us have the right to call a credit reporting agency and make an appointment to review our files. There may be incorrect information on file that is affecting our ability to receive credit. Sometimes there can be instances where minor systems problems may affect your credit ability without your knowledge. For example, when you apply for credit at any given organization, not only does the credit reporting agency provide a history for the requesting organization, it also tracks the number of times a credit check has been done on you. The higher the number of credit checks, the more difficult it becomes to obtain credit, as it appears that an individual is trying to pay one debt off by taking another debt on, or even worse, running up credit everywhere. Many times this can happen in error, like when one company, through its own systems error, conducts multiple credit checks on the same consumer.

The principle of being able to apply to have a credit error corrected applies to any organization that holds your personal information. They must, upon request, make personal files available for review. Typically, organizations have 30 days to make the file available and this should be communicated to the consumer as soon as possible to avoid any complaint to the Privacy Commissioner's office.

In most cases, real estate offices do not keep in their files any personal information that is already available in the client's lawyer's file. As a result, you should not receive many requests from customers to review their personal information. However, in the unlikely event that you do receive such a request, you should do your best to make certain the request is satisfied on a timely basis.

Principle 10 – Challenging Compliance
A consumer shall be able to address a challenge concerning compliance with the above principles to the designated accountable person or persons in the member office.

Managing this principle may well be the most important duty of your office's Privacy Officer. Privacy Officers must be empowered to address any questions or concerns raised by the public about your privacy policies, which will involve doing everything possible to address a consumer complaint.

Consumers are not required to approach an organization directly about a complaint before advising the Privacy Commissioner's office. Therefore, you should welcome any complaint that comes to you first as an opportunity to resolve the customer concern before it escalates to a formal review by the Commissioner's office. By complaining, customers are giving you the chance not only to solve their complaints, but also to develop procedures in your office to ensure that other customers do not suffer the same treatment. In this way, you can use the complaint as a positive means to make your privacy policies that much better going forward. Many successful organizations do the same thing by proactively soliciting complaints from their existing customer base, in order to nip any problem in the bud before it spreads to the rest of their customer base.

Principles 7, 8, 9, and 10 apply directly to Privacy Officers. These officers should be the ones to educate your staff about the importance of privacy and to educate your clients, too. The policy should always be available for review in your office and, for the reasons set out in our discussion of Principle 8, should be used as a marketing opportunity every time you meet with a potential customer. The Privacy Officer should also make available personal information files for review by consumers upon request and should be diligent in satisfying any customer complaint that comes into your organization about your privacy policies.

If you spend the proper amount of time training and educating your staff about your privacy obligations, you may actually see an increase in your business. More importantly, you should be able to avoid any potential complaints or legal challenges. Stay off any future Privacy Wheel of Misfortune.

ISSUES RELATING TO MORTGAGE BROKERS

The 10 principles of privacy are just as applicable to mortgage brokers as to agents. However, there are some points that apply specifically to the mortgage broker community.

Collection and Protection of Sensitive Personal Information
Mortgage brokers are in the business of collecting as much personal information as possible in order to qualify customers for the needed financing to complete their purchase and sale transactions. Because most of this information is sensitive, brokers should take even greater measures to protect it, including shredding any personal information that is to be destroyed.

Consent from Third Parties
Since most applicants are in fact consumers, they are not commercial enterprises when they provide any information, such as support payments from a spouse. It is thus arguable that since the applicant is authorized to submit this information to the mortgage broker, then the broker is also authorized to submit this together with the rest of the applicant information even though it is personal information about a third party spouse. Perhaps one could consider removing the name of the

third party spouse from the application, leaving only the notation that the applicant is in fact receiving this additional source of income. It would not be surprising if family law practitioners include a term in future separation or divorce proceedings such that spousal support is information that can be disclosed by the receiving spouse for the purpose of verifying income received by any third party, for the purpose of any loan or other application.

Passing Information on to Other Brokers or Lenders

Similar to Principle 2 regarding identifying purposes, so long as the purpose is identified to the consumer, then personal information can be passed on by the mortgage broker to other brokers or lenders. This purpose could easily be incorporated as part of the existing language whereby the broker obtains the consent of the applicant to conduct a credit check. Consent should be expanded to include the disclosure of any personal information to any other person required in order to successfully secure the financing requested by the applicant.

Soliciting Past Clients When Their Mortgage Renews

A practice has developed whereby some lenders check the mortgage details of consumers from the records at local land registry offices and then attempt to contact these consumers with marketing information as their mortgages are about to expire, in order to get them to transfer their mortgage. This method of contacting clients is very similar to the practice by some real estate agents of soliciting expired listings, which is a violation of the Privacy Act. Lenders will have to amend these practices going forward or they will be subject to potential privacy claims.

However, if the mortgage broker is marketing for renewal purposes to his existing customers because their mortgages are about to expire, I would consider this to be normal follow-up to the initial mortgage agreement. It can even be argued that the customer gave implied consent to this when he first entered into the mortgage application. Nevertheless, it makes sense, going forward, to include this purpose either in your mortgage application in accordance with Principle 2, or in your Mortgage Broker Privacy Policy, as mentioned under Principle 8.

Obtaining a Confidentiality Agreement from Lenders

I think there is a difference between lending institutions and private lenders in terms of the privacy policies adopted at each. It is important, whenever you are dealing with private lenders who may be likely to contact a customer, that you obtain a confidentiality agreement that they will also protect any personal information you may disclose to them. Some people may even want to obtain such an agreement from an institutional investor, but we can assume that they already have measures in place to protect customer information.

Passing Information on to the Buyer Agent

In order for a buyer broker to waive any condition regarding financing put in place by a buyer, it is prudent for the agent to request information in writing that the buyer has in fact been approved for the financing. For this reason, this permission should also be included as part of your privacy policy or included in your mortgage application. However, when buyers are pre-qualified for a mortgage, they may be reluctant for their agent to know the upper limit of this approval so that the agent does not disclose this value in the course of negotiations with the agent for the seller. There is no reason to disclose this information to a buyer agent without the express permission of the mortgage applicant.

Weisleder's Wisdom on . . . THE PRIVACY ACT

1. Prepare a privacy policy for your office.

2. Appoint a Privacy Officer in your office and ensure that they are responsible to educate the rest of your staff on the importance of complying with all Privacy Act obligations.

3. Indicate in your privacy policy that you will market the successful sale of your client's property.

4. Use your privacy policy as a marketing tool as soon as possible when you sign a client to a listing or buyer agent agreement.

5. Use confidentiality agreements whenever possible.

6. Ensure that your open house sign-in sheets and company newsletters have proper privacy language.

7. Do not let yourself be fooled by unscrupulous clients; you must still always disclose material information to the other parties in a transaction – this is not "private." Remember full disclosure principles.

8. Always deal with any complaint from the public as quickly and respectfully as possible, to avoid a claim to the Privacy Commissioner's office.

Risk Management

Many agents think, "It doesn't really matter if I make a mistake — that's why I carry insurance, to protect me. It is just the cost of doing business. And if my professional real estate council calls me onto the carpet for anything, I will just apologize and move on. They are a group of real estate professionals like me, so they will understand." Unfortunately, it is not that simple.

One of the main goals of this book is to help you avoid legal actions against you or involvement in a provincial real estate council discipline proceeding. In order to better illustrate the consequences, I want to take you through what occurs in a legal or discipline action involving real estate agents.

LEGAL PROCEEDINGS

"I went bankrupt twice in my life. The first time when I lost a case. The second time when I won." — Voltaire

Most people understand when they are contemplating bringing a civil proceeding against someone that the legal costs are going to end up being substantial. This alone is usually a sufficient deterrent to commencing legal proceedings. However, if you ask litigation lawyers what the subject matter is of most commercial litigation, they will tell you that a vast majority of cases involve real estate disputes. This is primarily due to the large sums of money involved in most of these transactions. Just consider that in the Toronto and Vancouver real estate markets, the sale of million dollar homes is a regular occurrence. Accordingly, if things go wrong, the amounts of money involved, unfortunately, justify legal proceedings.

The Legal Process

Here is a summary of what would probably take place if an action was brought against you as a result of a real estate transaction, including the time frames involved and the fees incurred.

Upon receiving a claim, you will experience a combination of surprise, shock, and indignation that someone would institute proceedings against you. Defence counsel I've spoken to who defend negligence actions against professionals say that most agents are ill-prepared for the consequences of a legal action, both professionally and emotionally.

Next, several negative effects kick in. Inevitably the broker is named as a party as well, meaning that this action will immediately affect your relationship with your broker. It will also affect your working relationship with other agents in your office. The real estate community is small, especially in smaller regions. Claimants speak to their neighbours, and soon your problems will become public knowledge, even before many of the legal papers have been filed. As the real estate agency business is largely a word-of-mouth referral business, this can have immediate repercussions on your ability to earn a living. (I have even heard of situations in which a legal action has torn apart an entire small-town church where both the complainant and the agent were members of the same congregation.)

It is one thing to be sued when someone slips on the ice

outside your home. It is quite another when someone questions your livelihood, alleging that you are negligent in what you do for a living, or even worse, that you have committed some sort of fraudulent action. Even if your immediate reaction is that the allegations contain no merit whatsoever, you will still feel a great deal of emotional turmoil. Most people in this situation take these kinds of allegations personally and, as such, seriously.

As you can see, the action itself has barely started, and yet your entire world has been turned upside down.

I watched with interest when Martha Stewart was interviewed after being sentenced in her own criminal proceeding. Here was a woman who was the queen of advice on almost everything related to domestic life, from cooking to decorating to raising children. Yet she was quite frank in admitting that there were no books or magazines with advice that could have adequately prepared her for the stress and the complexities of the legal process.

According to most errors and omissions policies, the agent and broker must report the claim to the insurance company as soon as possible. There is information on the RECO Web site regarding obtaining the Notice of Claim and instructions regarding where to forward all relevant information about the claim that has been made. This information will be used by the insurance adjuster as well as the lawyer who is appointed by the insurance company to act on your defence.

In some cases, the situation will be reviewed by the insurance adjuster after conducting an interview with the claimant as well as the agent involved. In order to avoid costly legal proceedings, the adjuster may recommend a settlement to the insurance company if the claim has merit and the damages are easily ascertained. However, if the claim is of a nuisance nature, or it is not clear as to liability or damages, then defence counsel will be retained to act on your behalf.

The lawyer will want to meet with you to review the allegations made in the claim and will need you to produce any documents, e-mails, or notes that you may have in your possession that relate to the claim. This may include any notes that you keep in your daily planner as well as your diary. You will be asked detailed questions by the lawyer as to what every notation means. Besides the fact that you may not remember what all the notations refer to, some of the material may be very embarrassing to you personally.

Most agents will be certain that they did not do or say anything wrong but will have little in the way of documentation to support their claims, due to the fact that they are generally working on many transactions at once and do not have the time to document everything. Most defence counsel who practise in this area relate that with virtually every claim made, there is a point in the process in which the defendant agent says, "Had I known this would happen, I would have written everything down," or "I wish I had taken notes about that."

The first interview as well as subsequent reviews of the statement of defence and any changes to it will probably take up to five working days of your time in preparation. This does not include any motions that may be brought to strike out some offensive paragraphs in the statement of claim that may not be relevant. In support of any motion, it is usual for the agent to have to file a supporting affidavit. It will take extra time to review the material before it is filed.

The other lawyer is also given time to cross-examine you on the subject matter of any affidavit that is filed. This will involve more preparation and then personal attendance for the actual cross-examination. The cross-examination is recorded and can be used later in both the upcoming motion and at trial. For any motion, add another three days of time that you will lose in preparation for and attendance of the cross-examination.

Did I mention the lack of sleep that you will have on the night before the examination, thinking about the questions that the lawyer is going to ask you? We are not even close to the actual court hearing, yet you have probably already lost two full weeks of time that could have been used productively in other ways.

The next main document that has to be prepared is the affidavit of documents, where both sides must provide a list of all the written documents that are to be produced at trial in support of their positions. For this document, you will be required to dig up everything you can find, including any e-mails that relate to the matter, any phone records that relate to conversations that may have been held on a specific date, and your own personal diaries.

Once the affidavit of documents is completed, then the lawyer for both sides has the opportunity to examine each party on what is called a discovery, in order to learn what the facts and legal positions are that each party will be relying on at trial and what documents will be brought in support of the position, so that there will be no surprises at trial.

Besides using this process to review everything that may be written in your own diary, the lawyer for the complainant will ask many detailed questions about all the training you have undergone and all the update courses, conferences, and seminars you have taken or attended. They are searching for a way to discredit your ability. Thankfully, most jurisdictions have continuing education requirements in order for agents to retain their licence and registration. Taking the proper training as well as ongoing training not only will equip you to deal with this ever-changing business, it also will provide you with a useful tool to defend any attack on your ability to do your job. In addition, the lawyer will ask for examples of your other transactions. They are looking for a negligent pattern that they can point to, for example, that you never document anything so there is a strong likelihood that you are confused or that you have been careless in previous transactions.

The discovery proceedings are also recorded and the information obtained can be introduced at the trial as well. In many cases, defence counsel will also request that the agent attend while the plaintiff (complainant) is being questioned, in the event that the defendant can assist counsel with any of the questions to be asked as a result of the responses given by the plaintiff. This process usually takes another full week.

Other motions can be brought between the discovery stage and the trial, which could result in further attendances by the parties to answer questions and sign affidavits in support.

The trial itself usually takes one to two weeks, depending on the complexity of the facts and the number of witnesses. The preparation for trial will usually take at least another week, as you will have to reread your examination for discovery to familiarize yourself with all that has taken place. The trial is often held three to four years after the initial claim has been filed, and the agent is expected to be at the trial at all times. The hours spent in court are often very exhausting. You should not expect to get any work done while a trial is in progress. By then you will be totally consumed by it.

Most agents involved in the process are amazed by the amount of paper that is generated in the case file. Even something as small as a "slope in the kitchen" (as we soon will see) could result in detailed structural engineering reports being prepared by experts who will also have to appear at trial to give evidence.

The total time you might spend on this matter is at least two full months, to say nothing of the stress of having this action hanging over your head for the entire three-to-four-year period. Can anyone really quantify the true amount that is lost by the agent as a result of this process, both from the money that could have been earned during those lost two months, and the loss of health as a result of the stress related to the lawsuit itself? For many years medical researchers and doctors have stated that stress directly and indirectly contributes to health problems, including heart disease and cancer.

There is also the possibility that the results of the action will become public knowledge, as all legal proceedings are public information. The case results could be discussed in a newspaper article or the case may appear on the Internet, resulting in negative publicity about you or your broker that will have a definite impact on future business. So much of our business is based on reputation and word-of-mouth referrals. Nothing could be worse for business than having a reputation of being involved in nasty court battles. It never matters to third parties who was right — just being involved carries a stigma.

The following is an actual case summary of proceedings against an agent, from the time the claim was issued until the matter was finally decided. The case was *Wood* v. *Lautenbach*, and the action commenced in 1998. The trial took place in the spring of 2004, six years later, and lasted four weeks.

The matter began simply enough. The property was listed by a seller who had lived in the property for several years. Some minor renovations had been done on the property. The buyer noticed the property after seeing a For Sale sign while driving by. They immediately contacted their agent because they wanted to see it.

The property had a slope in the kitchen that some witnesses said was visible when inspecting the house while others said it was not. In this case, the buyers and their agent did not notice the slope in the floor. Another buyer who had put in an offer at the same time did in fact notice the slope on their own. The slope was stated to be 11 inches from one end of the house to the other.

The buyer admitted that there was some discussion about having a home inspection but that they had finally determined not to do so. The buyer agent did not make a strong argument that a home inspection should be done.

The transaction closed. Sometime after closing, the property began to deteriorate. It turned out that the slope in the floor was the symptom of a problem with the foundation. Ultimately, some years after the transaction had closed, the house had to be demolished. The buyer claimed damages from the sellers, the listing and selling agents, and the town.

The issues at trial were whether the listing agent was aware of the defect, and thus had a duty to disclose it, and whether the buyer broker should have inspected the property more carefully to the point where they should have strongly recommended a home inspection.

The case began with a statement of claim being served in 1998. The trial was completed in the spring of 2004. The end result was that the buyer agent was held responsible for not recommending that the buyer conduct a home inspection, which would have uncovered the defect. The township was also held partially responsible for not ensuring that the house complied with the Ontario Building Code and for failing to conduct proper inspections during construction. Due to complicated expert engineering evidence required, the trial took 16 days. It is safe to say the legal fees exceeded the total value of this property. These six years of stress and costs could have been avoided if the parties had only taken the time to examine their respective duties to disclose and protect their respective clients.

In summary, here are the steps involved for the agent in the legal process.

- The agent must provide the insurer's lawyer with an initial report – a written synopsis of events that occurred – as well as all file documentation.
- The agent then has to meet or have a telephone conference with the lawyer regarding the facts that are in the synopsis, and may have to obtain further information.

• The agent has to review the defence prepared by the lawyer and provide any comments.

• The agent has to provide all documentation to be included in the affidavit of documents to be delivered to the plaintiff and will also have to attend personally to execute this affidavit of documents.

• Examinations for discovery require the agent's attendance for the purpose of giving evidence under oath while being questioned by lawyers adverse in interest, including the plaintiff's lawyer. The agent has to meet with the insurer's lawyer prior to the examination for discovery to prepare for it.

• Mediation is now generally compulsory and requires that the lawyers and the parties attend in an effort to resolve the matter out of court. Mediations are generally a minimum half-day and may take a full day. Prior to the mediation, the lawyer will provide the agent with a copy of the mediation brief for review and comment.

• The rules of civil procedure in legal actions also generally require that the parties attend a pre-trial settlement conference. This is similar to mediation but takes place before a judge. Again, there is an exchange of a pre-trial memorandum for review and comment by the agent prior to the session. Pre-trials are generally one hour in length and require the agent's attendance and participation.

• Preparation for trial could involve substantial time on the part of the agent in terms of gathering information for the lawyer and meeting with the lawyer, assisting in discussions with respect to retention of experts and review of their report, and, of course, giving evidence at trial. Trial requires attendance of the agent for the purposes of giving evidence, which includes cross-examination by lawyers adverse in interest in open court. Agents are also asked in many instances to remain in court to listen to other evidence that is material to the case, to provide any comments or other input.

Insurance Issues

Agents are correct that their or their broker's errors and omissions insurance policy is meant to protect them should they make a mistake in the course of a transaction. However, these policies should be examined to determine what in fact they do cover since all policies contain some exclusions.

For example, if an agent commits fraud in the course of a transaction, and it is proven, there will be no coverage. If fraud is alleged, the insurer will defend the action, but if the allegation of fraud is proven later at trial, then the costs will have to be paid by the agent and/or broker.

Furthermore, if the agent is involved in the transaction with a financial interest, either as a buyer or seller or in acting as a mortgage broker, then again there will be no coverage. That means the agent and/or the brokerage will have to pay the full legal costs to defend the action as well as the full amount of any judgment that is awarded, which can be prohibitive.

Many policies do not cover the agent for property damage. Consider a case in which an agent has not properly qualified a proposed tenant and this same tenant turns the property into a grow house, cultivating illicit marijuana for sale, with significant damages done to the property. An action may be brought against the agent for damages because the agent did not properly qualify the customer. The agent's errors and omissions policy will not cover this type of damage. The practice of most insurance companies is to decline to cover damages caused by illegal acts. Both brokers and agents should acquaint themselves well with the gaps and exclusions in their insurance policies so that, if necessary, they are able to purchase supplemental coverage.

Following receipt of an initial notice that a claim may be made or is being made, many agents would like to see the matter just go away as soon as possible. Some make the mistake of trying to call the person making the claim in an attempt to settle the matter before informing the insurance company. Doing this could have disastrous consequences. If you say anything in the course of your discussions that the insurer deems to have materially affected their ability to defend you, the insurer may deny coverage immediately and you will have to deal with the entire matter on your own.

Most agents indicate that they do not want to proceed to trial. The insurer, however, will not agree to resolve a matter if they are of the opinion that there is no liability. If the insured agent continues to insist on resolving the matter, it will be at their own expense.

Sometimes, the insurer may recommend that the matter be settled but the agent insured does not agree to settle, particularly when they feel that their own reputation will be detrimentally affected. In such a case, the insurer will end their involvement with the case and the agent will have to pay all costs from that date going forward. This includes the risk of paying the full damages if the matter does in fact proceed to court and the agent is unsuccessful.

There are other potential pitfalls with your insurance policy. One standard clause requires the giving of notice to the insurer as soon as a claim arises or circumstances arise that could result in a claim. A potential claim arises where the agent could "reasonably foresee" that his or her actions could give rise to a claim. If there is a problem with a closing of the transaction or if a complaint is made by someone about the agent's actions either before or after closing, this is the moment that the insurer will likely say that notice of the claim should have been provided to the insurer.

Agents, therefore, must understand the necessity of notifying their insurer of such potential claims immediately. The notice allows the insurer to make an investigation at an early stage when memories are the best and it can obtain the best factual account of what has occurred. It is also possible that the insurer may be able to repair the situation and keep expenses at a minimum.

Unfortunately, too many agents make the determination that they are not liable even when it is apparent that there is a problem. They just do not feel that they are the source of the problem and believe that it must arise out of someone else's actions. This type of person often goes into denial mode and fails to report the matter. Sometimes these agents try to assist their own clients by providing statements or affidavits to the client's lawyers. Agents should be very wary of this practice. They should refrain from providing statements or taking any steps to assist parties to a dispute without first consulting their insurer. Ultimately, any such statements may contain admissions of liability of the agent that may result in the insurer denying coverage to the agent later.

All insurance policies contain a cooperation clause, requiring the insured agent to attend all hearings, mediations, arbitrations, trials, and examinations, and to give evidence and assist in obtaining the attendance of other witnesses helpful to the case. While the agent may have insurance that will pay for the cost of the defence and any damages that are found by a court or in a settlement, the defence of such matters requires the agent's active participation as if the agent himself or herself was the party responsible for making the payments.

If the agent declines to participate and assist, the insurer may withdraw coverage, in which case the agent will have to take personal responsibility for the payment of the defence of the action and any damages.

Financial Involvement

Even when it is determined that you are covered by insurance, your financial involvement is far from over. To begin with, there is a $2,500 deductible, meaning that you will be required to pay the first $2,500 of any legal costs or damages that are determined against you. If it was as simple as a payment of $2,500, many agents might continue to be cavalier about the matter. But it becomes much more than that, even if you win and do not have to pay anything further; there are the costs of lost business, of sick days caused by stress, of loss of confidence in doing your job, and, in some cases, the loss of one's profession if the agent is banned from practising real estate.

Settle!

If, unfortunately, you do become involved in a legal proceeding, try to reach a settlement, and the earlier the better. As already mentioned, the very worst settlement is still preferable to the best legal position. Once a matter is settled, it is over, and since the terms are usually confidential, there is no negative publicity associated with it either. I have heard too many times the phrase, "It's not the money, it's the principle." Forget it. It's always about the money. And if you just factor in what it really costs you, in terms of time and stress, you are actually in a better financial position, in almost every situation, by settling.

However, because most court cases against agents will be defended by the agent's errors and omissions insurers, it may not be a simple matter to just settle the action. The insurer does not want to establish precedents that it is easy to just bring a claim against an agent and collect a quick settlement from the insurance company. The insurer may also feel that the claim has no merit and should thus be defended, all the while having regard to the legal fees that have to be paid to defend the case. It will likely not be the agent's decision alone whether to settle the matter. But, if you are in this position and have an opportunity to do so, urge that a settlement be made, so you can put the matter behind you.

RECO PROCEEDINGS

Many agents do not understand the role of RECO in the real estate profession. Accordingly, I would like to discuss briefly RECO's structure and mandate. (Much of what I say applies to the other provinces' real estate councils as well.)

The government of Ontario, by virtue of the Real Estate and Business Brokers Act, the Safety and Consumers Statutes Administration Act, and regulations under those Acts along with an agreement between the Ministry of Consumer and Commercial Relations and RECO, has established a set of guidelines giving powers to the real estate profession so that it has become, in many respects, self-governing, similar to the manner in which the legal profession is self-governing.

This power is not granted in a cavalier manner. RECO takes its responsibilities to the profession, the public, and the government very seriously. There is no desire by the real estate agent profession as a whole to be completely regulated by government officials who do not understand the business. In order to earn the trust of the profession, the government, and the public, great care must be taken to ensure that agents continue to receive proper and updated training so that the public interest is properly served. Furthermore, RECO must ensure that improper behaviour by agents or brokers is disciplined appropriately in order to deter other agents from this kind of behaviour and, more importantly, to continue to maintain the public trust. (A similar process and mandate is found in the Law Societies across Canada, which self-regulate the legal profession, both in educational and practical requirements as well as their own discipline proceedings.)

A person applying to become a broker or salesperson must first apply to the Registrar for registration. Terms of registration require continuing professional education and continued membership in RECO.

Contrary to a belief held by some agents and the public, RECO is not a collection agency that consumers can go to in order to collect amounts that they feel are owing to them by an agent or broker. If that is what a consumer wants, they can go through the legal proceedings noted above.

RECO has established a code of ethics for its members, not only to ensure that agents deal with each other in good faith, but also for the protection of the public interest. To enforce and ensure compliance with this code of ethics, RECO has created, through a by-law, a discipline committee whose members are appointed by the board. There is a full procedural scheme that goes into effect once a complaint has been made. There are different paths that a complaint can take once it is made, and each complaint is taken seriously by the committee.

If RECO determines that the complaint is related to a violation of its code of ethics or the Real Estate and Business Brokers Act, or if a member has breached a term of their membership in RECO, then it will proceed to deal with the matter.

RECO will first notify the person against whom the complaint was made, as well as that person's broker, if applicable, to give them the opportunity to respond, usually within a 15-day period. Many agents assume that every complaint goes to a discipline hearing. This is not the case at all. In fact, only a small percentage of the total number of complaints received actually goes through the process of a formal hearing. In the latest statistics obtained from RECO, for 2003, out of over 7,000 complaints that were received, only 51 discipline hearings were conducted.

Most of the matters are resolved in other ways, at the discretion of the manager who oversees each complaint. In determining the appropriate response, the manager will consider the seriousness of the allegations as well as the remedies that are available. He will also look to see whether this is the first time a complaint has been made against the agent or whether he is a repeat offender.

If the response is very detailed and explains the circumstances, and if the agent is cooperative with the manager investigating the matter, then the case may well be settled quickly by the agent agreeing to take additional educational courses and/or signing undertakings not to engage in the kind of activity complained of again. The matter may also be referred to alternate dispute resolution (ADR), in which the parties attempt to resolve the matter through mediation.

If a mediated solution is reached, then an agreed upon statement of facts or summary is presented to the RECO discipline committee for approval. The recommendations are generally approved in most cases. The additional good news is that in the mediation process, while the summary itself is made public, no mention is made of the names of the parties — which is very important when you think of the negative publicity associated with committee hearings. The results of these hearings, including the names of all agents and brokers, are posted on the RECO Web site for at least a two-year period. Any member of the public can take a look at these decisions by clicking on the Web site. This is also generally the same in all provinces of Canada, where similar boards operate and administer the real estate agent community.

Some would argue that because the information posted is personal information about an agent, RECO should not be permitted to publish the name of the agent who is involved in a legal proceeding. But RECO is not engaged in a commercial activity, as defined under the privacy legislation, and has declared by a by-law that these decisions can be made public. When agents become members of RECO, they agree to be bound by its by-laws, and RECO (and other provincial councils like it) is thereby in a position to publish the results of any discipline proceedings.

In a RECO proceeding, it doesn't matter whether the original complaint is made by a fellow agent or a member of the public — the "plaintiff" in the action is RECO. RECO brings the action and retains lawyers to act on its behalf. Any fine or penalty that is levied against an agent goes to RECO, to be used to support their costs and programs. None of this money is given to any complaining agent or consumer. If the matter is serious, it will usually proceed to a hearing. The process is faster than a typical legal action, but will still take approximately eight months from the time a complaint is received until the actual hearing takes place.

Initially a researcher is appointed to gather all facts related to the claim. The researcher then files a report, which is relied on by RECO in determining whether or not the matter should proceed to a hearing or whether it can be disposed of immediately or through the mediation process.

Once a matter is referred to the discipline committee, that committee still has discretion whether to proceed. The committee members are made up of realtors from the profession, who bring years of experience and understanding to their work. They are also conscious of their duty to the public and to the profession in general, to ensure that serious violations are dealt with in a manner that will foster confidence in the system. If the committee decides to proceed to a hearing, based on the report of the researcher, a Notice of Hearing is given to the agent against whom the complaint is made, at least 30 days before the hearing. The agent will be given the opportunity to review all evidence compiled by RECO for use in the hearing. This is similar to the discovery process in a legal proceeding, but is much less formal. The initial complainant, whether a consumer or another agent, will also have to attend the discipline hearing in person in order to give evidence.

The hearing is conducted in front of the three-member committee similar to a trial, with each party bringing their witnesses and the other side being given the opportunity to cross-examine any of the witnesses. Although there are grounds to appeal a decision, no new facts may be introduced on appeal. The agent would have to prove that there was a denial of natural justice, meaning that perhaps the committee was biased against him for personal or other reasons, in order to have a chance to succeed. There have been very few successful appeals. However, there have been cases in which the penalty given to the realtor has been reduced on appeal. In most cases where there is any possibility of a conflict of interest, such as if the committee member works in the same area as the agent being complained of, the committee member will declare the conflict in advance and not sit on that particular hearing.

The hearing could be avoided if the parties agree on a joint statement of facts with a recommended penalty. Although the committee is not bound to accept the recommended penalty, they do accept it in the majority of cases. Avoiding a hearing in this manner makes it more likely that your name will not be used in the decision that is published on the RECO Web site.

It is interesting to note that although an agent who initiates a complaint against another agent will have to appear as a witness at the hearing itself, this agent will not be identified in the decision that is posted on the RECO Web site. She is just referred to as "the buyer's agent," or "buyer broker," as the case may be. This is done so as not to discourage agents from bringing complaints in the first place for fear of appearing in any subsequent written decision. If the agent or member of the public that made the complaint fails to attend in person for the hearing, this may in fact lead to the case not being proven to the satisfaction of the committee. It is an element of the fairness of the proceedings themselves that the agent should have the opportunity to challenge, by way of cross-examination, the evidence that is being presented by the complainant. If that person refuses to appear in person and thus denies the defending agent this opportunity, then the agent will have a very good chance of succeeding in his defence.

Notwithstanding the foregoing, I do not advise an agent to try to spend substantial resources and time defending a position in the hopes that the complainant will not appear at the discipline hearing. This is much different than hoping that the policeman who gave you a traffic ticket does not show up for the trial. You now know all procedural steps that are involved in a RECO proceeding. Do your best to avoid the proceeding in its entirety by practising safely and following your real estate board's code of ethics. If, however, proceedings are commenced against you, it is advisable to follow the step-by-step guidelines in this chapter on how to deal with the process.

My advice, should you become involved in a RECO hearing, is the same as with legal proceedings in general. Use the initial response as your best opportunity to have this matter dealt with as soon as possible. Treat this very seriously and try to answer all allegations as clearly as possible. Be cooperative with any researcher who may be assigned to collect information. If you can resolve the situation by attending education courses, that is a great result. You can then put the matter behind you immediately.

If that is not the case, try to resolve the matter through mediation and the ADR process. This should result in a negotiated settlement that, while not ideal, still serves the purpose of having the matter finalized quickly while not having your name publicized negatively on the RECO Web site under discipline proceedings.

Should the matter be set down for trial, again I suggest that you try to settle through an agreed on statement of facts with a recommended penalty, rather than go through the uncertainty of a trial. Always listen to your legal advisers' recommendation regarding your chances for success.

The costs associated with a discipline committee proceeding

should also be considered. In every case that I have referred to where an agent is found to have been liable, they have had to pay the costs of the RECO prosecutor, which have ranged in the decisions from about $1,000 to $2,000. The agent must also pay for their own legal costs in defending themselves before the RECO discipline committee. It is interesting to note that in a few of the cases where the agent succeeded in the matter, the agent asked for RECO to pay the agent's legal costs. In most instances, RECO has declined to make this payment, so the net effect is that the agent in almost all cases will have to pay their own legal costs as well, which can amount to $5,000 or even $10,000. These costs will likely not be covered by your insurance policy, a further incentive to avoid being the subject of RECO proceedings.

PRIVACY ACT PROCEEDINGS

Although the Privacy Act is relatively new and we have seen few cases involving real estate firms in general, we must continue to take the privacy issues outlined in this book very seriously. As discussed in the previous chapter, a complaint can be made to the Privacy Commissioner's office very easily. It does not cost a consumer anything to file one. The result of any complaint can be a very time-consuming, stressful audit. It can even result in federal fines, penalties, and subsequent civil proceedings by a consumer.

It is thus important for your organization to take seriously any complaint received from a client or customer. View this as an opportunity, not an aggravation. If you are able to solve a customer's complaint, not only will you defuse a potential embarrassing situation, you will be able to establish guidelines in your office so that these kinds of complaints never occur again. Furthermore, the customer is likely to remain even more loyal to your organization in the future and will be more likely to refer your company to others.

If you are not able, however, to solve the concern and the complaint is forwarded to the Privacy Commissioner's office, cooperate immediately with the Commissioner's representatives. Take great care in preparing any response to allegations made. Try to give the Commissioner's office the time to interview any applicable people in your organization, and ensure that your own privacy policy is available for the Commissioner's office to review.

As we all become more familiar with this legislation, it is important for us to remember that the Privacy Commissioner's office will try, to the extent possible, to mediate the situation between an agent and a consumer who has lodged a complaint. One of the best ways to resolve the matter is to demonstrate that you have taken the steps to ensure that this kind of behaviour does not recur, through the more complete incorporation of a privacy policy as well as educational requirements in this regard by all of your agents and administrative staff.

Forewarned
Is Forearmed
The 14 Steps of Success

The goal of any real estate professional is to create long-lasting, satisfied customers who return to use your services in the future, and recommend you to their friends. By following the principles set out in this book, not only will you stay out of potentially negative legal, discipline, or Privacy Act proceedings, you will also achieve your main objective of loyal customer relationships.

Here is a short summary of some basic principles to remember in your everyday real estate practice in order to avoid disciplinary or legal actions and increase your success.

1. Practise full disclosure

In everything that you do, remember the principle of full and complete disclosure no matter who you are representing. Disclose everything to your client and encourage your client to disclose everything material to the other party to the transaction. Be wary of any customer who is not willing to disclose matters that you suspect will cause problems for buyers. Your disclosure obligation begins as soon as you meet your client and continues right up until the property is sold and the transaction is completed.

2. Be prepared at your first customer meeting

There is a lot of truth to how much you can gain on a first impression with someone, whether in your personal or business relationships. Whether it is a listing presentation or a buyer agency meeting, being properly prepared serves many purposes. First, it ensures that you obtain all the required information to get started on your agency relationship. Second, it helps your client understand your relationship and what services you will be providing. Third, it helps your client begin to trust you, seeing that you consider them to be important and are treating them accordingly.

3. Get the contact numbers

At your initial client meeting, obtain all contact numbers for the client, including phone, cell phone, and fax numbers and e-mail addresses. Insert these immediately into your own contact list. This will make it easier for you to reach this customer and to have a record of any important communication.

4. Listen to your customer

No two customers are alike. All have different needs, whether they are sellers or buyers. Everyone has emotional as well as physical needs in a typical home purchase. You must begin to understand all of these needs right away. The best way is to ask a lot of open-ended questions and then just listen. It's not important to impress your customers with how much knowledge you have about the business — they expect this. Rather, it is important that you listen to their needs. This demonstrates immediately that you care, and it will be very unlikely for a customer to try to cheat you out of a commission later if you have treated them this way from the beginning of the relationship.

Make notes as to what the customer wants. For example, the seller may not want to have traditional open houses, or the buyer may only want to live in a particular area. Do not judge anyone as a result of any request. Besides writing the notes down, repeat back to the customer what it is that you heard. This further demonstrates that you are listening to their concerns.

5. Take notes of all instructions and conversations
Whenever something is very important, it is advisable to try to confirm the instructions via e-mail, as it can be done very quickly and then printed later for a permanent record. It is critical for you to make notes in your diary, daily planner, or personal digital assistant of all such conversations as well. These will be extremely helpful should disputes arise later.

6. Follow through with all commitments
Once you make a commitment to a client, you must follow through with it. This can include checking the zoning on a property, the ability to obtain a building permit, the quality or quantity of water from an existing well, or concerns about septic systems. What's more, you should then let the customer know that you have completed the task. Try to get confirmation from the customer that the commitment has been fulfilled and then make a note of it.

7. Be careful
Take your time when completing offers or listings. Most errors occur as a result of working too quickly and carelessly. Obtain written confirmation where possible for every important fact that is to be included on the mls listing. Ensure that you look at a copy of the deed itself to verify ownership, check a current tax bill to verify the taxes, and find a current survey to confirm the lot measurements. Fill out the spis form with your seller. Review the lawyer's reporting letter for any other defects in the property and then disclose them to any buyer. As a buyer

agent, always review the SPIS form with your buyer if it is available. Be careful when drafting any condition, to ensure that your client is properly protected.

8. Keep track of all important dates

Ensure that all important dates in a transaction are noted, especially condition waiver dates, as these are usually critical to the legal enforceability of the transaction.

9. Keep your customers informed

Follow up with your customers regularly. This practice permits you to convey the impression that they are important to you and also enables you to hear if anything new has arisen that may affect the listing or the transaction.

10. Do it the same way every time

Once you set up your own process as to how you sign up and explain the documents to your customers, be sure to do it the same way every time. Following the same pattern will also be invaluable to you as proof that you did do something if it is later disputed.

11. Refer to others for advice, when needed

Never hesitate to refer your clients to a lawyer for advice, at any stage in the transaction. Many discipline proceedings have gone in favour of agents who have been able to demonstrate that when an issue arose that affected the transaction materially, they advised the client to seek independent legal counsel. The fact, in some cases, that the client refused to follow this advice did not hurt the agents' position.

12. Stock training materials

Ensure that there is a proper training manual in your office, with guidelines for all important office procedures, including advertising guidelines.

13. Establish a mentor system

Try to establish a mentor system for every new agent so that there is proper supervision on everything they work on for at least the first six months of their practice.

14. Live your brand

Your personal reputation is your own brand image. Protect it at all costs as it is the source of all your referral business. Treat all customers, fellow agents, and office staff respectfully and professionally.

Seller Property
Information Statement

Seller Property Information Statement
Residential

Form 220
for use in the Province of Ontario

ANSWERS MUST BE COMPLETE AND ACCURATE This statement is designed in part to protect Sellers by establishing that correct information concerning the property is being provided to buyers. All of the information contained herein is provided by the Sellers to the broker/sales representative. Any person who is in receipt of and utilizes this Statement acknowledges and agrees that **the information is being provided for information purposes only and is not a warranty as to the matters recited hereinafter even if attached to an Agreement of Purchase and Sale.** The broker/sales representative shall not be held responsible for the accuracy of any information contained herein.

BUYERS MUST STILL MAKE THEIR OWN ENQUIRIES Buyers must still make their own enquiries notwithstanding the information contained on this statement. Each question and answer must be considered and where necessary, keeping in mind that the Sellers' knowledge of the property may be incomplete, additional information can be requested from the Sellers or from an independent source such as the municipality. Buyers can hire an independent inspector to examine the property to determine whether defects exist and to provide an estimate of the cost of repairing problems that have been identified. **This statement does not provide information on psychological stigmas that may be associated with a property.**

For the purposes of this Seller Property Information Statement, a "Seller" includes a landlord or a prospective landlord and a "buyer" includes a tenant, or a prospective tenant.

PROPERTY:	**SELLER(S) TO INITIAL EACH APPLICABLE BOX**			
SELLER(S):				
GENERAL:	YES	NO	UNKNOWN	NOT APPLICABLE
1. (a) I have owned the property for....................................years.				
(b) I have occupied the property from..to...........................				
2. Does any other party have an ownership, spousal, or other interest in the property?				
3. Is the property subject to first right of refusal, option, lease, rental agreement or other listing?				
4. If the Seller owns adjoining land, has a consent to sever been obtained within the last 2 years?				
5. Are there any encroachments, registered easements, or rights-of-way?				
6. (a) Is there a plan of Survey? Date of survey..				
(b) Does the survey show the current location of all buildings, improvements, easements, encroachments and rights-of-way?				
7. Are there any disputes concerning the boundaries of the property?				
8. What is the zoning on the subject property?..				
9. Does the subject property comply with the zoning? If not, is it legal non-conforming?..				
10. Are there any pending real estate developments, projects or applications for rezoning in the neighbourhood?				
11. Are there any restrictive covenants that run with the land?				
12. Are there any drainage restrictions?				
13. Are there any local levies or unusual taxes being charged at the present time or contemplated? If so, at what cost? ....Expiry date................................				
14. Have you received any notice, claim, work order or deficiency notice affecting the property from any person or any public body?				
15. Are there any public projects planned for the immediate area? Eg: road widenings, new highways, expropriations etc.				
16. Is the property connected to municipal water and sewer? If not, Schedule 222 must be completed.				
17. (a) Are there any current or pending Heritage designations for the property?				
(b) Is the property in an area designated as Heritage?				
18. Are there any conditional sales contracts, leases, or service contracts? eg: furnace, alarm system, hot water tank, propane tank, etc. Are they assignable or will they be discharged?..................................				
19. Are there any defects in any appliances or equipment included with the property?				
20. Do you know the approximate age of the building(s)? Age...................Any additions: Age........................				
21. Are there any past or pending claims under the Tarion Warranty Corporation (formerly ONHWP)? Tarion Warranty Corporation/ONHWP Registration No..				
22. Will the sale of this property be subject to GST?				

ADDITIONAL COMMENTS:...
....
....

ENVIRONMENTAL:	YES	NO	UNKNOWN	NOT APPLICABLE
1. Are you aware of possible environmental problems or soil contamination of any kind on the property or in the immediate area? Eg: toxic waste, underground gasoline or fuel tanks etc.				
2. Are there any existing or proposed waste dumps, disposal sites or land fills in the immediate area?				
3. Is the property subject to flooding?				
4. Is the property under the jurisdiction of any Conservation Authority or Commission?				
5. Are you aware of any excessive erosion, settling, slippage, sliding or other soil problems?				
6. Does the property have any abandoned well(s)?				
7. (a) Is there a fuel oil tank on the property? If yes, complete the following:				
☐ Underground. Date for required upgrading or removal....................................				
☐ Aboveground. Age of tank........................... Date of last inspection...............................				
(b) Does the fuel oil tank comply with the Technical Standards and Safety Authority requirements and any other requirements for fuel to be delivered?				
8. Has the use of the property ever been for the growth or manufacture of illegal substances?				

IMPROVEMENTS AND STRUCTURAL:	YES	NO	UNKNOWN	NOT APPLICABLE
1. Are you aware of any structural problems?				
2. (a) Have you made any renovations, additions or improvements to the property?				
(b) Was a building permit obtained?				
(c) Has the final building inspection been approved or has a final occupancy permit been obtained?				
3. To the best of your knowledge have the building(s) ever contained ureaformaldehyde insulation?				
4. (a) Are you aware of any deficiencies or non-compliance with the Ontario Fire Code?				
(b) Is your property equipped with operational smoke detectors?				
(c) Is the property equipped with operational carbon monoxide detectors?				
5. (a) Is the woodstove(s)/chimney(s)/fireplace(s)/insert(s) in good working order?				
(b) Has the wood energy system been inspected and approved? Approval Authority...............................				
6. Are you aware of any problems with the central air conditioning or heating system?				
7. Are you aware of any moisture and/or water problems?				
8. Are you aware of any damage due to wind, fire, water, insects, termites, rodents, pets or wood rot?				
9. Are you aware of any roof leakage or unrepaired damage? Age of roof covering if known......................				
10. (a) Are you aware of any problems with the electrical system? Size of service...................................				
(b) Type of wiring: ☐ copper ☐ aluminium ☐ knob-and-tube ☐ other................................				
11. Are you aware of any problems with the plumbing system?				
12. Is there any lead or galvanized metal plumbing on the property?				
13. Are you aware of any problems with the swimming pool, sauna, hot tub or jet bathtub?				
14. Is the outdoor lawn sprinkler system in working order?				
15. What is under the carpeting?..				
16. Is there a home inspection report available? Date of Report....................................				

ADDITIONAL COMMENTS:...
....
....

Schedule(s) attached hereto and forming part of this Statement include:..

THE SELLERS STATE THAT THE ABOVE INFORMATION IS TRUE, BASED ON THEIR CURRENT ACTUAL KNOWLEDGE AS OF THE DATE BELOW. ANY IMPORTANT CHANGES TO THIS INFORMATION KNOWN TO THE SELLERS WILL BE DISCLOSED BY THE SELLERS PRIOR TO CLOSING. SELLERS ARE RESPONSIBLE FOR THE ACCURACY OF ALL ANSWERS. SELLERS FURTHER AGREE TO INDEMNIFY AND HOLD THE BROKER HARMLESS FROM ANY LIABILITY INCURRED AS A RESULT OF ANY BUYER RELYING ON THIS INFORMATION. THE SELLERS HEREBY AUTHORIZE THAT A COPY OF THIS SELLER PROPERTY INFORMATION STATEMENT BE DELIVERED BY THEIR AGENT OR REPRESENTATIVE TO PROSPECTIVE BUYERS OR THEIR AGENTS OR REPRESENTATIVES. THE SELLERS HEREBY ACKNOWLEDGE RECEIPT OF A TRUE COPY OF THIS STATEMENT.

....   DATE..
(Seller)

....   DATE..
(Seller)

I acknowledge that the information provided herein is not warranted and hereby acknowledge receipt of a copy of the above information including any applicable **Schedule(s)**.

....   DATE..
(Buyer or Authorized Representative)

....   DATE..
(Buyer)

OREA Ontario Real Estate Association

Seller Property Information Statement
Schedule for Condominium

Form 221
for use in the Province of Ontario

This Schedule is attached to and forms part of the Seller Property Information Statement for:

PROPERTY:..

SELLER(S)..

CONDOMINIUM CORPORATION:	YES	NO	UNKNOWN	NOT APPLICABLE
1. (a) Condominium maintenance fee $...				
(b) Condominium fee includes:				
(c) Cost for amenities not included in maintenance fee $...................................				
Details				
2. Are there any special assessments approved or contemplated?				
3. Have you received any written notice of lawsuit(s) pending?				
4. Have you been informed of any notices, claims, work orders or deficiency notices affecting the common elements received from any person or any public body?				
5. (a) Has a reserve fund study been completed? Date of Study.................				
(b) Approximate amount of reserve fund as of last notification $....................				
6. (a) Are there any restrictions on the use of the property? e.g. pets, renovations				
(b) Are there any restrictions on renting the property? e.g. minimum term				
7. (a) If any renovations, additions or improvements were made to the unit and/or common elements, was approval of the Condominium Corporation obtained?				
(b) Is approval of any prospective buyer required by the Condominium Corporation?				
(c) Are any other approvals required by the Condominium Corporation or Property Manager? If yes, specify:				
(d) Name of Property Management Company				
8. Are there any pending rule or by-law amendments which may alter or restrict the uses of the property?				
9. Is the condominium registered?				
10. Parking: Number of Spaces .... ☐ Owned ☐ Exclusive Use ☐ Leased or Licensed				
11. Locker:... ☐ Owned ☐ Exclusive Use				
12. (a) Amenities: ☐ Pool ☐ Sauna ☐ Exercise Room ☐ Meeting/Party Room ☐ Boat Docking ☐ Guest Parking ☐ Other........................				
(b) Are you aware of any problems with any of the common element amenities? If yes, specify:				

ADDITIONAL COMMENTS:...
....
....
....
....
....

   Form 221   01/2004   **Page 1 of 1**

Seller Property Information Statement

Form 222

Schedule for Water Supply, Waste Disposal, Access and Shoreline *for use in the Province of Ontario*

This Schedule is attached to and forms part of the Seller Property Information Statement for:

PROPERTY:...

SELLER(S)..

WATER SUPPLY AND WASTE DISPOSAL:	YES	NO	UNKNOWN	NOT APPLICABLE
1. (a) What is your water source? ☐ Municipal ☐ Drilled ☐ Bored ☐ Dug ☐ Lake ☐ Community ☐ Shared ☐ Other...				
(b) If your water source is Community/Shared, is there a transferrable written agreement?				
(c) Are you aware of any problem re: quantity of water?				
(d) Are you aware of any problems re: quality of water?				
(e) Do you have any water treatment devices?...............................				
(f) Is your water system operable year round? Heated lines? ☐ Yes ☐ No				
(g) Date and result of most recent water test....................................				
(h) Are any documents available for the well? If yes, specify				
(i) Does the property have any abandoned well(s)?				
2. (a) What kind of sewage disposal system services the property? ☐ Municipal ☐ Septic tank with tile bed ☐ Holding tank ☐ Other..........				
(b) Are you aware of any problems with the sewage system? Date septic/holding tank last pumped............................ Age of system..................................				
(c) What documentation for the sewage system is available? ☐ Use Permit ☐ Location Sketch ☐ Maintenance Records ☐ Inspection Certificate ☐ Other................................				
3. Are the well(s), water line(s) and waste disposal system(s) within the boundaries of the subject property?				

ACCESS AND SHORELINE:	YES	NO	UNKNOWN	NOT APPLICABLE
1. (a) Is property access by municipal road? If yes; ☐ Open all year ☐ Seasonally open				
(b) Is the property serviced by a private road? Cost $.. per year.				
2. If your access is across private property, access is: ☐ Right of way ☐ Deeded ☐ Other .... Cost $.. per year				
3. (a) If water access only, access is: ☐ Deeded ☐ Leased ☐ Other........................				
(b) Water access cost of: Parking $................................. Dock $................................. per year				
4. (a) Is the original Shore Road Allowance owned?				
(b) Are there any pending applications for shoreline improvement?				
(c) Are there any disputes concerning the shoreline or improvements on the shoreline?				
(d) Are there any structures or docks on the original Shore Road Allowance?				
(e) Is the original Road Allowance included in the lot size?				
5. Does the boundary of the property extend beyond the water line? If yes, explain				

ADDITIONAL COMMENTS:...

....

....

Sample Privacy Policy

"Privacy Policy"
(Firm Name)

Policy on the Collection, Use, and Disclosure of Personal Information

1. Objective and Scope of Policy

(Firm Name) is committed to respecting your privacy and has prepared this Policy to inform you of our policy and practices concerning the collection, use, and disclosure of Personal Information.

This policy governs Personal Information collected from and about:

(a) individuals who are or may become Clients of (Firm Name), and

(b) individuals or organizations with whom (Firm Name) works.

Using contractual or other arrangements, (Firm Name) shall ensure that agents, contractors, or third party service providers, who may receive Personal Information in the course of providing services to (Firm Name) as part of our delivery of real estate services, protect that Personal Information in a manner consistent with the principles articulated in this Policy.

This Policy does not cover aggregated data from which the identity of an individual cannot be determined. (Firm Name) retains the right to use aggregated data in any way that it determines appropriate.

In the event of questions about (i) access to your Personal Information; (ii) (Firm Name)'s collection, use, management, or disclosure of Personal Information; or (iii) this Policy, please contact:

(Name or Title, address, e-mail address, telephone number)

_____

_____

_____

_____

2. The Collection, Use, and Disclosure of Personal Information
For the purpose of this Policy:

"Client" means an individual who may purchase or has purchased (Firm Name) real estate or services to buy real estate;

"Personal Information" means any information, recorded in any form, about an identified individual, or an individual whose identity may be inferred or determined from such information. Your provision of Personal Information to (Firm Name) means that you agree and consent that we may collect, use, and disclose your Personal Information in accordance with this Privacy Policy. If you do not agree with these terms, you are requested not to provide any Personal Information to (Firm Name) or a broker or sales representative working with (Firm Name). Unfortunately, certain services can only be offered if you provide Personal Information and consequently, if you choose not to provide us with any required Personal Information, (Firm Name) may not be able to offer you those services.

This office only collects Personal Information necessary to effectively market and sell the property of sellers; to locate, assess, and qualify properties for buyers; to market the successful sale of property completed on behalf of sellers and buyers; and to otherwise provide professional and competent real estate services to Clients.

(Firm Name), Brokers, or sales representatives may use Personal Information for commission management purposes (e.g., commission financing, commission dispute resolution).

(Firm Name)'s use of Personal Information is limited to these purposes. (Firm Name) does not sell, trade, barter, or exchange for consideration any Personal Information it has obtained. Unless permitted by Law, no Personal Information is collected about an individual without first obtaining the consent of the individual to the collection, use, and dissemination of that information.

Personal Information will be collected, to the extent possible, directly from the individual concerned.

(Firm Name) does not knowingly collect Personal Information from anyone under the age of 18, especially children under 13, and does not use such information if (Firm Name) discovers that it is being provided by a minor.

Personal Information may also be transferred to another company in the event of a change of ownership of all or part of (Firm Name).

(Firm Name) may disclose Personal Information of Clients to organizations that perform services on its behalf. This will only be done if such organizations agree to use such information solely for the purposes of providing services to (Firm Name) and, with respect to that information, to act in a manner consistent with this Policy.

Please note that there are circumstances where the use and/or disclosure of Personal Information may be justified or permitted or where (Firm Name) is obliged to disclose information without consent. Such circumstances may include:

(a) where required by law or by order or requirement of any court, administrative agency, or other governmental tribunal;
(b) where (Firm Name) believes, upon reasonable grounds, that it is necessary to protect the rights, privacy, safety, or property of an identifiable person or group;
(c) where it is necessary to establish or collect monies owing to (Firm Name);
(d) where it is necessary to permit (Firm Name) to pursue available remedies or limit any damages that (Firm Name) may sustain; or
(e) where the information is public.

Where obliged or permitted to disclose information without consent, (Firm Name) will not disclose more information than is required.

3. Accuracy

(Firm Name) endeavours to ensure that any Personal Information provided by Clients and in its possession is as accurate, current, and complete as necessary for the purposes for which (Firm Name) uses those data. Information contained in files that have been closed is not actively updated or maintained.

4. Retention

(Firm Name) retains Personal Information as long as (Firm Name) believes it is necessary to fulfill the purpose for which it was collected and (Firm Name)'s legal or business requirements.

5. Security

(Firm Name) endeavours to maintain adequate physical, procedural, and technical security with respect to its offices and information storage facilities so as to prevent any loss, misuse, unauthorized access, disclosure, or modification of Personal Information.

(Firm Name) further protects Personal Information by restricting access to it to those Employees and Contractors that the management of (Firm Name) has determined need to know that information in order that (Firm Name) may provide services to Clients.

6. Access to Personal Information

(Firm Name) permits access to and review of Personal Information held by (Firm Name) about an individual by the individual concerned.

If an individual believes that any Personal Information concerning the individual is not correct, that person may request an amendment of that information by sending a request to the person indicated in Section 1 of this Policy. (Firm Name) reserves the right not to change any Personal Information but will append any alternative text the individual concerned believes appropriate. An individual may also request that (Firm Name) delete an individual's Personal Information from (Firm Name)'s system and records where not required to be retained by (Firm Name). Personal Information may continue to reside in (Firm Name)'s systems after deletion. Individuals, therefore, should not expect that their Personal Information would be completely removed from (Firm Name)'s systems in response to an accepted request for deletion.

(Firm Name) reserves the right to decline access to Personal Information where the information requested:

a) would disclose the Personal Information of another individual or of a deceased individual;

b) would disclose confidential business information that may harm (Firm Name) or the competitive position of a third party;

c) is subject to solicitor-client or litigation privilege;

d) could reasonably result in: (i) serious harm to the treatment or recovery of the individual concerned; (ii) serious emotional harm to the individual or another individual; or (iii) serious bodily harm to another individual;

e) may harm, or interfere with, law enforcement activities and other investigative or regulatory functions of a body authorized by statute to perform such functions;

f) is not readily retrievable and the burden or cost of providing it would be disproportionate to the nature or value of the information; or

g) does not exist, is not held, or cannot be found by (Firm Name).

Where information will not or cannot be disclosed, the individual making the request will be provided with the reasons for non-disclosure.

Where information will be disclosed, (Firm Name) will endeavour to provide the information in question within a reasonable time and no later than 30 days following the request.

(Firm Name) will not respond to repetitious or vexatious requests for access. In determining whether a request is repetitious or vexatious, it will consider such factors as the frequency with which the information is amended, the purpose for which the information is used, and the nature of the information.

To guard against fraudulent requests for access, (Firm Name) will require sufficient information to allow it to confirm the identity of the person making the request before granting access or making corrections.

7. Amendment of Practices and this Policy

This Policy statement is in effect as of (insert date). (Firm Name) will from time to time review and revise its privacy practices and this Policy. In the event of any amendment, an appropriate notice will be communicated to Clients and others in an appropriate manner.

Confidentiality Provisions
When Giving out Comparative Market Analysis

"Confidential Information" means information regarding the sale price of homes that will be used on a comparison basis only for the purpose of determining the value of the subject property being purchased/sold, as typically contained in a comparative market analysis.

During the course of the relationship between the agent and the client, the agent may disclose to the client Confidential Information solely for the purpose of the client determining the value to either list or put in an offer to purchase a subject property.

The client agrees to protect and safeguard the Confidential Information, not to disclose it to any third party other than financial or legal advisers of the client, and only to use it for the purposes outlined in this agreement.

The obligations under this agreement shall survive the termination of the listing/buyer agency agreement between the parties.

The client will indemnify the agent for any damages suffered by the agent caused by a breach of the client of their obligations under this agreement.

APPENDIX D

Receipt of
Privacy Policy

To: (Name of Real Estate Company)

The undersigned acknowledges having received, reviewed, and accepted the terms of the (Name of Realtor) Privacy Policy.

Index